ASTROLOGY

PLAIN & SIMPLE

Cass & Janie Jackson

THE ONLY BOOK YOU'LL EVER NEED

Previously published in 2005 by Zambezi Publishing Limited, Devon, UK.

Cover design by Jim Warner
Interior designed by Kathryn Sky-Peck

Hampton Roads Publishing Company, Inc.
Charlottesville, VA 22906
Distributed by Red Wheel/Weiser, LLC
www.redwheelweiser.com

Sign up for our newsletter and special offers by going to
www.redwheelweiser.com/newsletter/

ISBN: 978-1-57174-747-1

Library of Congress Cataloging-in-Publication Data available upon request

Printed in Canada

MAR

10 9 8 7 6 5 4 3 2 1

TABLE OF CONTENTS

Dedicated to our grandchildren—

Alastair, Carin, and Christopher

Thomas and Rebecca

Joby and Amy

Jazmin and Samantha

INTRODUCTION

"There is nothing simple about astrology," a friend told us. "All those measurements and degrees and logarithms—what's simple about it?"

It's true that over the centuries a certain mystique has built up around the science of the stars. It's equally true that there is now a resurgence of interest in astrology, and many would-be stargazers are seeking simple do-it-yourself instructions to help demystify the art of chart interpretation. *Astrology Plain and Simple* provides an answer to that quest.

You almost certainly know your Sun sign—and that is the most important astrological factor of all. Once you know the Sun signs of your friends and relations, you'll be able to read them like a book. Add to this Sun sign knowledge some idea of the effect of the planets on each sign and you'll understand why these people act as they do. This information in itself is more than sufficient for you to begin to understand what makes people tick.

If, after absorbing this amount of know-how, you become so hooked on astrology that you want to learn more, this book goes on to explain houses, aspects, transits—and a variety of other strange-sounding words. Sure, you'll need to put on your thinking cap, but providing you're not expecting to become Astrologer Royal or to set up in a lucrative business, you'll find everything you need to know. If you're the ambitious type (Aries or Leo perhaps?), you can easily find out more by delving into other books, or surfing the web, or attending courses. Quite literally—the sky's the limit.

PISCES
ARIES
TAURUS
GEMINI
CANCER
LEO
VIRGO
LIBRA
SCORPIO
SAGITTARIUS
CAPRICORN
AQUARIUS

The Zodiac

1

The astrological signs that begin with Aries and continue through Pisces are known collectively as the signs of the zodiac. These names are derived from groups of stars that we know as constellations. Most of these constellations were thought to represent animals—though you need a vivid imagination to see them in the night sky—hence the names: Aries, the ram, Taurus, the bull, Cancer, the crab, and so on. The Greeks called these constellations *zodiakos kyklos*—"circles of animals"—which translated into the English word "zodiac." The table on page 5 lists all the zodiacal signs in order, and their corresponding animal or symbol.

Imagine standing on top of the world, able to see the sky all round you. The zodiac would form a belt around you, with the constellations in the order in which they are normally encountered—Aries, Taurus, Gemini, and so on around to Pisces, which completes the circle.

The ancients realized that the Sun, as it traversed the sky, passed through every zodiac sign each year, before starting its round again. Records were made of the dates on which the Sun passed from one constellation to the next. Although they vary by a few days each year, the dates for each sign are typically as shown in the table on page 5.

♈	Aries	Ram	March 21—April 19
♉	Taurus	Bull	April 20—May 20
♊	Gemini	Twins	May 21—June 21
♋	Cancer	Crab	June 22—July 22
♌	Leo	Lion	July 23—August 22
♍	Virgo	Virgin	August 23—September 22
♎	Libra	Scales	September 23—October 23
♏	Scorpio	Scorpion	October 24—November 21
♐	Sagittarius	Archer	November 22—December 21
♑	Capricorn	Goat	December 22—January 19
♒	Aquarius	Water Bearer	January 20—February 18
♓	Pisces	Fishes	February 19—March 20

This divided the year up very nicely into twelve almost equal sections. The astrological year always starts with Aries, which begins around March 21, the spring equinox—a time when the days and nights are of equal length. This was also the start of the ancient Roman calendar, and while other calendars have come and gone, this one has stuck fast, as far as astrology is concerned.

Imagine that you are again standing on top of the earth, with the zodiac slowly moving around you. You are standing at the center of a disc, of which the zodiac forms the border. Dotted about on this disc are the planets that also appear to be revolving round the earth.

From our point of view on earth, the Sun appears to pass though each zodiac sign during the course of the year. This orbit is so regular that anyone can find their Sun sign by looking at their horoscope in the newspaper, or at the dates listed in the table on page 5. Although this works well for most people, the Sun doesn't change sign at exactly the same time or even on the same day of each year. This means that those who were born on the cusp (that is to say, on the border) of two Sun signs might not be sure which sign is truly theirs.

Astrologers also use the Moon and the planets of the solar system in their studies. A Moon sign will show your inner, emotional nature. (You will be able to find the position of your Moon on the day of your birth in chapter 6.) The planets represent the cosmic energies that influence your basic character. Depending on the time you were born, the planets occupy different zodiac signs in your astrological chart and thus affect your personality. We will go into more detail about the planets in chapter 4.

The rising sign (also known as the ascendant), is the sign of the zodiac that was rising above the horizon at your time of birth. It is another very important factor since it says something about how other people perceive you. The rising sign is connected to the time of day you were born. All twelve zodiac signs will rise during the course of 24 hours. Unfortunately, they are not broken into nice, neat 2-hour blocks of time. Don't worry: this book will help you find your rising sign in chapter 5!

At some point you will probably want a professional astrological chart made that lists every feature with absolute accuracy. Check out websites such as *www.sashafenton.com* or *www.astro.com* to find out how you can obtain a free horoscope and how to buy extremely inexpensive astrology software. In addition, you may want to visit your local astrologer. He or she will be able to point out more complex features in your chart, as well as help you understand what is going on in your life at a particular time.

PISCES
ARIES
TAURUS
GEMINI
CANCER
LEO
VIRGO
LIBRA
SCORPIO
SAGITTARIUS
CAPRICORN
AQUARIUS

The Signs of the Zodiac

The twelve signs of the zodiac influence the planets as they pass through them, directing their qualities into the different behavioral patterns that we recognize as personality traits.

For example, when we speak of someone being born under the sign of Libra we mean that, at their date of birth, the Sun was passing through the zodiac sign of Libra. Such a person will likely exhibit the characteristics and traits that are traditionally associated with a Libran Sun sign.

The sign of Aries is always considered as the first sign of the zodiac. This is because the Sun enters the sign of Aries at the time of the spring equinox, which is around March 21, when the days and nights are of equal length. The exact dates and times for the start of each sign vary from year to year, so all astrology books can only give approximate dates.

The main characteristics for each of the Sun signs can be found in the following pages.

ARIES

Sign of the Ram

Gender:	**Masculine**
Element:	**Fire**
Quality:	**Cardinal**
Ruling planet:	**Mars**
Temperament:	**Extrovert**

If you were born under the sign of Aries, you're very likely to be gregarious and dynamic. Your friends will see you as a natural-born leader who has to be in charge of any undertaking. If, for any reason, you're forced to take a back seat, you're likely to be up and away in search of another more exciting project.

You have an almost childlike enthusiasm for anything new. The ram's motto is "Me first!" If you're a typical Aries, you'll be convinced that your life's purpose is to lead others in the way they should go. Some of you see life as a game in which you have to call the shots, or a competition that you have to win.

Certainly, you're not one to let an opportunity of any kind pass you by. You'll seize it with both hands, confident of immediate success. If things don't go your way, you'll probably fly into a temper. Rams on the rampage are to be avoided, as they can be violent when roused. Fortunately for others—and for your blood pressure—you quickly forget your bad moods and behave as though they never happened.

You are a positive character, strong-willed, optimistic, and full of energy. You're energetic and courageous and take life's problems in stride without complaint.

TAURUS

Sign of the Bull

Gender:	Feminine
Element:	Earth
Quality:	Fixed
Ruling planet:	Venus
Temperament:	Introvert

In marked contrast to impulsive Aries, those born under the sign of Taurus will be steadfast and determined. You are patient and completely reliable. Once you have embarked on a course of action, you are reluctant to deviate from it. This is the positive side of your determination. Others may call you stubborn. Risky undertakings don't appeal to you. You prefer to lay back and let the rest of the world get on with things. Though you would hotly deny that you are lazy, you do tend to be self-indulgent; you definitely like an easy time and a great social life, or a working life that has elements of socializing as part of it.

Linked with this is your aversion to any form of change, which is why you often remain in an unsatisfactory situation. You're not happy with it, but feel that change involves risk and you don't like taking chances. The odd thing is that, although you'll accept being stuck in a rut, you're easily bored. Material possessions are important to you. Obtaining them may indeed be one of the driving forces of your life and can lead to unaccustomed hard work. It could be said that your greatest aims are to enjoy yourself and have a good life. You're certainly highly sensual and few people realize that, if necessary, you can be one of the most down-to-earth, conservative people of the zodiac.

GEMINI

Sign of the Twins

Gender:	Masculine
Element:	Air
Quality:	Mutable
Ruling planet:	Mercury
Temperament:	Extrovert

With a Gemini Sun, you will be adaptable and versatile, making your dexterity a valuable asset. You're forever curious, always looking for ways to improve yourself and your life. This avid interest in anything and everything may encourage you to take on too many projects at any one time, meaning you'll deal with each one in a rather superficial manner. You're always full of ideas, but seldom put them into practice because your interest peters out once you've discovered the ins and outs. Although you have a great deal of mental and physical energy, you tend to dissipate this force by being unstable and inconsistent.

Others love your quick wit, fluent conversation, and spontaneity. No party is ever dull if a Gemini is at the center of activity. Few people know how indecisive, uneasy, and nervous you feel behind that cloak of gaiety. Some may see through your superficiality and realize that you can be both cunning and calculating. Even so, your quick wits and conversational skills enable you to talk yourself out of any difficult situation.

Your Sun sign—the twins—manifests in your duality, making you seem eccentric or at least unconventional. This is not necessarily a negative trait. Some of the world's greatest inventions were created by Geminis with their practical yet intellectual approach. This duality also makes itself apparent in your emotional make-up. Others may see this as vacillation. The truth is that your feelings are not determined by any deep-seated emotions. They depend entirely on how you feel at any one particular moment.

CANCER

Sign of the Crab

Gender:	**Feminine**
Element:	**Water**
Quality:	**Cardinal**
Ruling planet:	**The Moon**
Temperament:	**Introvert**

You are one of the most sensitive signs of the zodiac, though you try—usually without success—to hide this aspect of your nature. What else you hide beneath that Cancerian shell nobody knows. You tend to be reclusive, allowing others into your life only on a need-to-know basis. In fact, you have an extremely strong streak of secretiveness in your make-up.

When problems arise in your life, you will do almost anything to avoid facing them. In this respect, you're a cross between an ostrich and a crab. First, you stick your head in the sand, pretending that if you can't see the problem it will go away. Then, when forced to face facts, you will do so in the most indirect way possible.

Your vivid imagination often surprises people. Your sudden hunches can be valuable to you in your business life, as can your characteristic shrewdness and inborn flair for commerce. Although you may start up in business for yourself, you are not well suited to working alone, preferring to have a partner. This works well until that partner appears to let you down or slight you in any way because you never forgive or forget. This sort of situation could result in one of the moods of dark depression to which you are prone. In turn, this will make your outlook even more negative than usual.

Despite your natural shyness, you are a very caring and affectionate person who can be quite emotional and protective toward the people you love.

LEO

Sign of the Lion

Gender:	**Masculine**
Element:	**Fire**
Quality:	**Fixed**
Ruling planet:	**The Sun**
Temperament:	**Extrovert**

True to your birth sign, you exhibit all the majestic leonine qualities. The words that best describe you are regal, noble, dignified, proud, and self-confident. You are completely aware of these attributes, realizing that even if you don't possess them to the full, you have a duty to act as though you do. Your behavior is always flamboyant, and this is reflected in your speech and your clothing. Not only does your exuberance carry you along, it is contagious and others feel swept along with you. You are always the leader, which you feel is only right and proper. Leo, after all, is king of the jungle, and you expect to lead, even if your particular jungle is decidedly urban.

You will take on almost any task and, once committed, you'll stick with it until the job is completed. No project is too big for you to attempt. You tend to see the overall picture, without bothering over minor details. In this respect, you are one of the most creative people of the zodiac. You set high standards for yourself and expect the same from others, not hesitating to show your disappointment if they are unable to keep up with you. Your imposing attitude may give the impression that Leo is grand and unapproachable. This is not so. Your family and friends know you to be both tender and lighthearted. This tenderness can become manifest when you've been hurt, though you will be careful not to let others see your pain.

Others sometimes see you as arrogant, but your charm is such that you get away with it.

VIRGO

Sign of the Virgin

Gender:	Feminine
Element:	Earth
Quality:	Mutable
Ruling planet:	Mercury
Temperament:	Introvert

If you were born under the sign of Virgo, your perfectionism will probably irritate everyone you know. This won't bother you, because you believe that your meticulous attention to detail is only right and proper. Your redeeming feature is that you are as critical of yourself as you are of others. Although you may appear unemotional, your greatest satisfaction in life comes from helping others. Few people realize this because your shyness and lack of self-esteem keep you out of the limelight.

You can be obsessive about health and hygiene, or you may spend energy worrying about whether your house will be swept away in a flood (even if it is on a hill), or you may have other obsessions. Old-time astrology books used to harp on about how neat and tidy you are, but that just isn't true. You can live and work in a mess, but you know where everything is and you go ballistic if someone interferes with your stuff or moves it. You may be fastidious about your diet though, and people consider you a very fussy eater.

On the mental level, you are as precise as you are practical—possibly even more so. You'd never take on a job without first being sure that you know and understand the smallest details of the operation. If there are any gaps in your knowledge you're quite prepared to spend some time—and indeed, you may insist on—acquiring the missing information. Only then will you apply yourself wholeheartedly to the task in hand, fulfilling your reputation of being the hardest worker in the zodiac.

LIBRA

Sign of the Scales

Gender:	Masculine
Element:	Air
Quality:	Cardinal
Ruling planet:	Venus
Temperament:	Extrovert

Born under the sign of Libra, you are almost certainly a diplomat with a strong predilection for justice. Fairness is an obsession with you and you simply cannot accept the fact that, at times, life is not fair. This can make you appear to be a poor loser. Your diplomacy makes you the supreme arbiter since you can always see both sides of any argument. On the one hand, you love to keep everything well balanced, harmonious, and orderly, but on the other hand you also love to debate and argue. The scales of justice are your symbol and you can argue like a lawyer when the mood takes hold of you.

You find it difficult to make decisions; you'd rather sit on the fence, keeping everything in balance. This type of situation makes some Librans extremely vulnerable and easily influenced. Those who recognize this weakness may take advantage of you. However, Libra is a cardinal sign, and as such, you are disinclined to live according to other people's rules or do anything other than exactly what pleases you.

Your manners are perfect. You are charming and courteous and you can be the guru of good taste. You are the perfect host. You love to entertain and be entertained, and you enjoy good food, good wine, and good company; companionship, in fact, is an integral part of your life. Even so, you do occasionally need periods of peace and quiet in order to recharge your batteries and restore the balance in your own life.

Strangely, although you are forever mindful of fair play, you are not above bending the rules when it suits you. On such occasions, you claim that you are adding a little extra "corrective" weight to one side of the scales in order to maintain perfect balance.

SCORPIO

Sign of the Scorpion

Gender:	Feminine
Element:	Water
Quality:	Fixed
Ruling planet:	Pluto
Temperament:	Introvert

Scorpios often look for some form of security in a world they find intimidating. Your inner lack of confidence gives rise to the notion that you are unfriendly and obsessive. The truth is that you are inclined to be secretive and others may see you as neurotic. You can overcome these problems only when you are in full control of your life—and that doesn't often happen to any of us.

Your need for security means that you are forever seeking to wrap up your current situation and start a new life. Sometimes this is not possible, whereupon you may suddenly change your lifestyle for no apparent reason. When your powerful emotions are kept under control, you are tender and devoted, dazzling others with your magnetic personality. However, if anyone displeases you, you can be unforgiving and vindictive. Scorpio never forgets an injury.

Your worst fault is that you are so self-absorbed that you use up other people and wear them out. You may drain them financially, demand that they keep on traveling when they are exhausted, or go on and on about yourself and demand that they focus their minds day and night on your most minute decision or problem until the other person wants to scream.

Traditionally, yours is the most highly sexed sign of the zodiac. You are certainly passionate in all areas of life, including your work and play. Everything you do is undertaken with the utmost intensity. It must also be said that you make a faithful and passionate lover. With your charismatic personality, you will not lack willing partners.

You are strongly intuitive, probably due to your deeply reflective and spiritual nature, and you use this quality to successfully analyze and solve problems for others, even if you cannot solve your own.

SAGITTARIUS

Sign of the Archer

Gender:	**Masculine**
Element:	**Fire**
Quality:	**Mutable**
Ruling planet:	**Jupiter**
Temperament:	**Extrovert**

If you were born when the Sun was in Sagittarius, you are endowed with boundless enthusiasm. You like to appear confident to others, but you feel far from confident within yourself. Your energies are often channeled into sport and you may be a devotee of outdoor games. You also love to travel. This is also a reflection of your need for freedom, both mental and physical. All the greatest explorers have some aspect of Sagittarius in their make-up. You feel complete and able to breathe properly only when you are out in the world. If you are in any way restricted, you become moody and miserable, but as long as you have your freedom, you are the perpetual optimist. You choose jobs that take you from place to place or that allow you to choose your own hours.

You have an enquiring mind and love a mental challenge, being prepared to delve deeply into any subject that interests you. Indeed, you have no time for what you see as the trivial issues in life or other people's problems. This is evidenced by one topic that is a perpetual source of interest to you: Why are we here?

These stimuli are necessary to your nature. Without them, you become bored and then your negative side comes out. This mainly manifests as restlessness and inconsistency in your behavior and a very sharp and hurtful tongue.

In addition to having a probing mind, you are quite intuitive and can often immediately see the grand design that eludes others. Unfortunately, you are capable of producing more schemes in your head than you can ever bring to fruition. Nevertheless, you enjoy your grand ambitions and hate to be tied down by routine. Sagittarius likes nothing better than to embark on some new and outlandish project.

CAPRICORN

Sign of the Goat

Gender:	Feminine
Element:	Earth
Quality:	Cardinal
Ruling planet:	Saturn
Temperament:	Introvert

Like the goat, Capricorn is sure-footed, but in an abstract, cerebral sense. There's nothing indecisive about you. You are very self-disciplined, able to plan and then achieve your self-imposed long-term goals, and these objectives will be sound, sensible, and practical ones. As a child, you were undoubtedly reputed to have an old head on young shoulders. Strangely, though, you were probably a slow developer. You have complete faith in your own abilities and the possibility of failure simply does not exist for you.

You don't attempt to hide your ambition to obtain some form of appreciation and acknowledgment in society as a whole. In your drive to reach the top, you can even be ruthless with anyone who obstructs your progress. Like the goat, you'll keep on climbing until you reach the top.

Although you work hard and long, you are not blessed with a quick mind and you hate to be hurried. As a consequence, you prefer to work in a situation where you can plod along at your own steady pace. Avoid at all costs any situation in which you are expected to come up with speedy answers to complicated questions. This will lead only to depression and disillusionment. If this happens, you will retreat to the security and stability of you own home and family—the mainstays of your life.

AQUARIUS

Sign of the Water Bearer

Gender:	Masculine
Element:	Air
Quality:	Fixed
Ruling planet:	Uranus
Temperament:	Extrovert

Why do others see you as being stubborn? You know what is right and stick to your principles. What's wrong with that? You are certainly forthright in proclaiming your ideals. You can't understand why others won't join you in fighting for your rights, justice, freedom, peace—or whatever cause you are supporting this week. Your radical views and the fervor with which you project them may exclude you from a large portion of society, which sees you as an eccentric weirdo. This doesn't bother you. It's *they* who are out of step. You'll have no hesitation in joining organizations, leading protest marches, and organizing demonstrations for what you consider to be worthy causes. You value freedom of expression and will fight for it above all else. This is the Aquarian nature, and there's nothing you can do to change it. What your critics don't know is that beneath this radical exterior there cowers an insecure individual who genuinely cares for others, and for humanity as a whole.

Although you are only too willing to express your views on your objectives, you are reluctant to expose your essential self. As a result, you make few friendships. Those friendships you do make are shallow, because you treat all strangers with caution. Additionally, your touch-me-not manner does not exactly invite closeness. You don't want anyone to stifle your personal freedom. This attitude unfortunately fights against the formation of close relationships in which a partner might come to appreciate your loyal and loving nature.

PISCES

Sign of the Fishes

Gender:	**Feminine**
Element:	**Water**
Quality:	**Mutable**
Ruling planet:	**Neptune**
Temperament:	**Introvert**

Pisceans are among the most sensitive of individuals, instinctively aware of the emotions of others and always willing to help those in trouble. Your intuition goes beyond the normal. You simply "know" when things are wrong and you don't wait to be asked for help. You'll do almost anything to maintain the status quo as long as it keeps the rest of the world happy. To escape a confrontation you'll give way and accept other people's ideas simply for peace and quiet.

When you're alone, you drift into a fantasy world where everything is perfect. This is the escape mechanism you need when you realize that you are not living in utopia and life is not as peaceful and serene as you would like it to be.

You tend to magnify your fears and problems and can become quite irrational; hence your need to get away and immerse yourself in dreams. This escape can take many forms. Many writers, poets, and actors are Pisceans who unconsciously use their art as a means of escape from reality. Sadly, some Pisceans tend to go even further in their flight from the harshness of life and seek release through alcohol or drugs.

Because you want everything to be perfect, you will often romanticize a situation and put on rose-colored glasses. In one-to-one situations, this can be dangerous. It is all too easy for you to fall in love with love, rather than with the object of your affections.

Now that you've been introduced to the qualities of each zodiac sign, you have the most basic building block to understanding your astrological chart. But there is so much more to understanding what makes you tick! Let's continue to explore *Astrology Plain and Simple*.

PISCES
ARIES
TAURUS
GEMINI
CANCER
LEO
VIRGO
LIBRA
SCORPIO
SAGITTARIUS
CAPRICORN
AQUARIUS

3

Genders, Elements, and Qualities

The signs of the zodiac fall into three different categories: the genders, the elements, and the qualities. Each of these categories gives us more information about the characteristics of the signs of the zodiac.

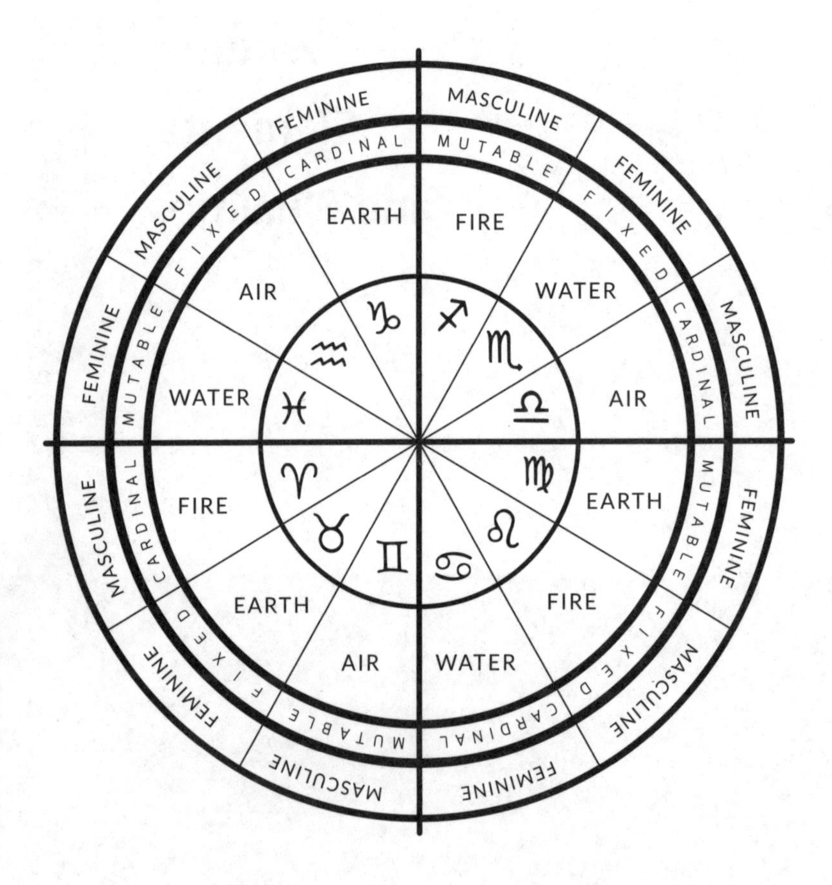

The Genders

The first category is called "the genders" and its characteristics are masculine/feminine, positive/negative, or even yang/yin. In this book, we will use the terms "masculine" and "feminine." These terms just describe the energies of the signs; none are considered better or worse than any others. The signs alternate as follows:

Aries	**Masculine**
Taurus	**Feminine**
Gemini	**Masculine**
Cancer	**Feminine**
Leo	**Masculine**
Virgo	**Feminine**
Libra	**Masculine**
Scorpio	**Feminine**
Sagittarius	**Masculine**
Capricorn	**Feminine**
Aquarius	**Masculine**
Pisces	**Feminine**

Masculine signs tend to be extroverts, while the feminine signs are introverts.

Looking at the signs in greater depth, we see that the masculine signs are active and outgoing, with a tendency to be assertive or even aggressive. Anyone born under a masculine sign is likely to be impulsive and to enjoy taking chances. They will have a bold, optimistic attitude and are likely to prefer active pursuits rather than sedentary ones. They are the courageous "doers" of the zodiac who will work or fight to achieve something. They are the yang energy, without which there would be no progress or development, just an ongoing Stone Age way of life.

Feminine signs are retiring and contemplative, tending to keep themselves to themselves. They have a caring nature and are considerate of others. Gambling of any kind is not their scene, and they are unlikely to take risks. Before making any move, they will carefully evaluate the situation. These are the nurturers who work away quietly, ensuring that fields are tilled and children are cared for. Without this yin energy, the world and its people would not have endured as long as they have.

The Elements

The second category concerns the elements of fire, earth, air, and water. The elements represent the four basic natures as recognized by the earliest astrologers.

The elements of fire, earth, air, and water are found in the signs consecutively, as follows:

Fire	Earth	Air	Water
Aries	Taurus	Gemini	Cancer
Leo	Virgo	Libra	Scorpio
Sagittarius	Capricorn	Aquarius	Pisces

The fire signs are Aries, Leo, and Sagittarius. These people are full of fire. They are get-up-and-go personalities who demand immediate action. If you were born in a fire sign, you will never be a bystander. Whatever the enterprise, you will be an enthusiastic participant, immediately taking the lead. This fervor is apparent in everything you do and you always live life to the full. You do have a spiritual side to your nature and this is reflected in your obvious joy in living. Fire signs are individualists, usually completely self-sufficient. Beware of your tendency to be over-impulsive. It could cause you difficulties.

The earth signs are Taurus, Virgo, and Capricorn, a group of extremely practical people. It's possible that the expression "down to earth" derived from this group. You'll weigh all the pros and cons before entering into any project and you won't rush into anything. Like the earth itself, you are solid and dependable. You possess a great deal of common sense and are endlessly patient. You are also some of the most methodical people of the zodiac. Unrealistic people or ideas irritate you, and your approach to any situation is strictly practical.

The air signs are Gemini, Libra, and Aquarius. These people are intellectual and great communicators. Born under one of these signs you will be intuitive as well as inquisitive, and will constantly come up with new ideas. You are never satisfied with the status quo and always want to improve everything. Your extrovert nature, combined with your intellect, means that you want to communicate your ideas to as many people as possible. As a result, you are likely to have dozens of friends. You are straightforward and outspoken, with no time for those who are overly cautious or ultrasensitive. Try not to become too enthusiastic about your own ideas. People who don't understand them may claim you are talking a lot of hot air.

The water signs are Cancer, Scorpio, and Pisces. This group is capable of great compassion and sensitivity. You are quick to sum up other people, often at first meeting, and you are usually right. This is because you "feel" things rather than observe them. Despite your sensitivity toward others, you are remarkably cynical about yourself and your abilities. In fact, you prefer your ideas to be put into practice by someone else, just as water takes the shape of the vessel that contains it. You're artistic, love music, dance, and poetry, but detest rowdy gatherings and noisy people. These drain your energy and leave you feeling exhausted. As a result, people may sometimes regard you as something of a wet blanket or a spoil-sport.

The Qualities

The third category divides the signs of the zodiac into the qualities of cardinal, fixed, and mutable. Taking the signs in turn, starting with Aries, you will see that the qualities are three signs apart. They each exhibit common features.

Cardinal	Fixed	Mutable
Aries	Taurus	Gemini
Cancer	Leo	Virgo
Libra	Scorpio	Sagittarius
Capricorn	Aquarius	Pisces

The cardinal qualities of Aries, Cancer, Libra, and Capricorn apply to those people who are primarily outgoing and enterprising. If you have a cardinal Sun sign, you are a person of action—a doer rather than a thinker—and tend to be determined in your attitude. This innate quality also predisposes you to restlessness. You're fantastic at organizing others, but often appear to be highly disorganized yourself.

The fixed qualities of Taurus, Leo, Scorpio, and Aquarius apply to those people who tend to be resistant to change. If this sounds as if you, a fixed sign, may be a stick-in-the mud, it could also indicate that you are faithful and persevering. You like to find yourself in a stable situation or help to create one if it does not already exist. You may not be a great initiator, but once started on a project you'll see it through to completion.

The mutable qualities of Gemini, Virgo, Sagittarius, and Pisces are found in people who are adaptable by nature. As a mutable sign, you're always willing to serve others, either by working in a service industry or agency, or simply as a person who goes around fixing things. This in no way implies that you are a drudge or that you will occupy a menial position. Even the President of the United States serves his country. You are versatile and you can adapt to almost any circumstance, which may be why so many of you move from one country or lifestyle to another. Where the fixed and cardinal qualities tend to stick with their own ideas, mutable people can always see both sides of any situation and act accordingly.

PISCES
ARIES
TAURUS
GEMINI
CANCER
LEO
VIRGO
LIBRA
SCORPIO
SAGITTARIUS
CAPRICORN
AQUARIUS

4

The Planets

Astrologically speaking, the term "planets" refers to the ten heavenly bodies that affect our horoscopes. These are not all planets; the Sun and Moon are actually luminaries. But in astrology, the Sun, Moon, Mercury, Venus, Mars, Jupiter, Saturn, Uranus, Neptune, and Pluto are all referred to as planets for the sake of convenience. In astrological charts, they are represented by symbols that are known as glyphs.

Your birth chart will show the positions of all the planets in relation to each other. The planets in your chart represent the cosmic energies that influence your basic character. We all know our Sun sign—the position of the Sun in the zodiac at the time we were born. It must be remembered, though, that the Sun alone is not responsible for all our characteristics. At the time of our birth, the planets each occupy a different position in our charts—hence the diversity of human nature. Each planet's energies are modified by its position in the zodiac—not only do the planets occupy a sign, but they occupy a "house" as well. We will delve into the meanings of the houses in chapter 7. The sign as well as the house will influence the energy of each planet.

In this section, we will look at each of the nine planets and what energies they symbolize. Understanding these energies, as well as the energy of your Sun sign, will enable you to understand all the forces that influence your character.

THE SUN

life force, creativity, basic personality

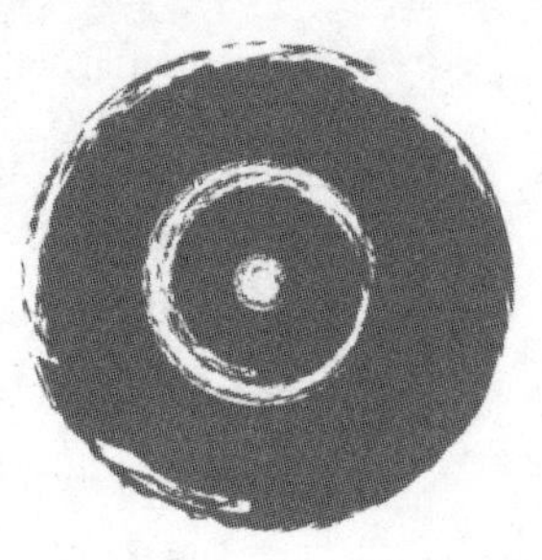

The Sun, without which there would be no life and which is at the center of our solar system, has the most effect on our personality. It is the largest of the astrological bodies and has the greatest influence, outweighing the effects of all the other factors in your chart. The Sun's position in your birth chart is the dominating factor, indicating your potential. Throughout your life, this position will influence your character and the way in which you express yourself. Where the Sun is found in your chart is where you will want to shine. The Sun represents your innermost identity. It is the symbol of the ego. It influences your basic attitude to life and your sense of individuality, your willpower, your creative energy, and your vitality.

The Sun travels in a complete circuit through the zodiac each year, staying in each of the twelve signs for approximately one month. The sign that it is in when you were born (your Sun sign) indicates how you will express your identity. For example, if the Sun was in Libra when you were born, you will exhibit Libran characteristics; that is, you will express your identity with harmony and diplomacy, as these are the keywords for Libra.

The house that your Sun occupies shows where your energies will be put into effect. You will identify strongly with the practical matters associated with this house. If the Sun is in your fourth house, you will express your identity through your family and home life because these are the keywords primarily associated with the fourth house.

The Sun's strong effects on your character are not usually felt until you attain full maturity—round about your 30th year. Until then, the Moon—its sign and house—usually has most effect on your behavior.

THE MOON

emotions, psychic energy, the subconscious

The Moon, our nearest planet, has the second most noticeable influence on our life. Its position in the zodiac at the time you were born defines your involuntary emotional reaction to any given situation. The Moon represents your true inner self. It reflects the female principle (yin)—mother, wife, daughter, and women in general—as well as feminine attributes of development and fertility.

The Moon also is responsible for a certain inertia that makes you at the least conservative, and at the most lethargic. If the Moon is strong in your chart, you will prefer to maintain the status quo and preserve everything that is familiar to you. The Moon is the symbol of the emotions, which it affects in every way, from your understanding of and reaction to others, as well as your feelings about your environment. The Moon also determines your needs regarding the giving and receiving of emotional support. These reactions are unconscious or inborn, revealing the clear influence of the Moon on your behavior and your instincts. The position of the Moon in your chart will show you where you are liable to encounter emotional swings.

The Moon moves through all twelve signs of the zodiac *in each month*, thus staying only two or three days in each sign. The speediness with which the Moon moves through the signs of the zodiac should give you some insight into the nature of your quickly changing moods and emotions! Women in particular are sensitive to the fluctuating influence of this feminine planet, since the menses typically follow a 28 day lunar cycle.

The sign that the Moon was in when you were born is your Moon sign and will indicate how you will react to and deal with your emotional needs. Thus if the Moon was in the sign of Aquarius when you were born you will tend to keep your emotional problems to yourself and deal with them in an unconventional way, as these are Aquarian characteristics.

The house that the Moon occupied when you were born will show where you are likely to look for increased emotional assurance. Thus, if your Moon is located in the eleventh house you will seek emotional security through your friends and acquaintances (keywords for the eleventh house) rather than through your family.

MERCURY

mental energy, communication

Mercury was the winged messenger of the Gods. This planet is related to your ability to communicate, to work, to duties, supervision of others, and health. Mercury has no gender, and it can reveal itself in either masculine or feminine characteristics.

This planet is connected with communication of all kinds. It also relates to your contacts with your friends and siblings, all of which are maintained by some form of communication. It is associated, too, with the way that your mind works and is the symbol of your reasoning ability. Mercury is often known as the trickster. Those who come under its influence are always capable of living by their wits, quite often on the fringes of society. The Mercurial influence on your nature means that you spend a great deal of your energy in thinking and talking. Mobile phones were made for Mercury types—the people who spend hours on the phone and then complain that they get nothing done, or who walk and talk, or even talk and drive at the same time.

Because Mercury was a messenger, the planet also influences your urge to travel. This doesn't necessarily mean that you'll circle the globe. Your journeys may be only to work or play, but a strong

Mercury influence in your chart indicates that you will certainly enjoy travel in some form.

Mercury can indicate the way your put your mind to work, to the kind of work that suits you, and to the way you interact with others or supervise them in your place of work. Health is another Mercury connection, so the kind of health problems you have might relate to Mercury, as would your attitude to health matters.

Check your birth chart to find in which sign Mercury is found. This position will affect the way you communicate. It will also reveal in which area your mental abilities are situated. Thus if your Mercury is in the sign of Scorpio, you will communicate with intensity and passion, as these are the keywords associated with Scorpio.

The house that Mercury occupies in your natal chart will show you the area in which your communicative flair is best engaged. If, for example, it is in the sixth house, then you will communicate best in your work or through service to the community, as work and service are characteristics of the sixth house.

VENUS

love, harmony, the feminine aspect

Venus is the planet associated with love and beauty. It is named after the Roman goddess of love. It represents your personal magnetism and your power to attract, as well as your wish for emotional harmony. Venus is associated with those aspects of your life that you most value. Its position in your chart will also indicate the type of personal relationships that you will make. Venus is not only connected with love in the erotic, sexual sense. It also encompasses your love of the arts, music, and the appreciation of beauty, as well as your need to give and receive warmth and affection. Your passion for beauty and luxury will no doubt be reflected in your home. There are times when you will be tempted to spend money on lavish items that you cannot afford.

Venus influences your choice of partner. If Venus is strong in your chart, you will be drawn to someone whose beauty is widely acknowledged, an outer beauty not simply in the eye of the beholder. Money will come easily to you, giving you the opportunity to make a beautiful home, and to buy beautiful things of all kinds.

Be aware that Venus can have its negative side. Should it be badly placed in your chart, it can express itself with hostility and ill will. A poor Venus makes it hard for you to make friends and somehow you tend to become the victim of bullies. It can mean that you don't have much luck with money or that you lose out in a divorce battle when love (Venus) turns into a battle over who owns what (Mars).

Venus is also associated with all that is feminine in your life—mother, sisters, friends, and the way in which you relate to women in general.

The sign occupied by Venus when you were born will indicate how you express your love. For example—Venus in Sagittarius suggests that you will exhibit your inborn traits through your love of freedom and tolerance, the key Sagittarian characteristics.

The house that Venus occupies in your birth chart will show where your loving energies will be put into effect. If, for example, Venus is in your seventh house, then you are fortunate. This is the house related to marriage and one-to-one partnerships on a personal level.

MARS

power, physical energy, strength

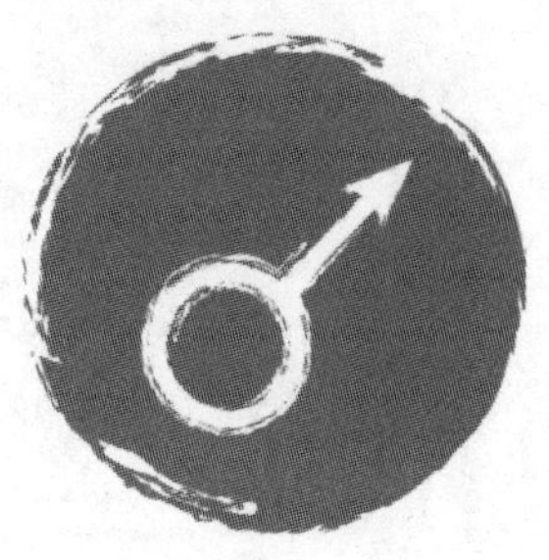

Mars takes its name from the god of war. Hence, Mars is associated with power, masculinity, and personal drive. Mars represents your fighting instinct and the animal side of your nature. At a less aggressive level, this could be described as your never-say-die attitude. If Mars is strong in your chart, you will meet all challenges bravely; however, as this is natural to you, you won't see yourself as particularly courageous. For you, this is the normal way to deal with any situation—boldly and with speed. At the highest level, you will be prepared—perhaps literally—to die honorably for your cause. Even if you're not willing to go that far, you will at least be ready to defend your beliefs and opinions and to protect what is yours.

Mars is also strongly connected with your sex drive. In any passionate relationship, the partner with the strongest Mars will dominate the sexual side of the relationship. It is interesting to note that whenever illustrations show Mars absorbed in an amorous adventure, he is still wearing his armor—always ready for war. The implication here is that you should expect fireworks, however romantic your Martian partner may be.

Mars represents male characteristics and yang energy, and is related to father, brothers, husbands, and men in general. In a man's chart, Mars will influence his attitude toward other males; in a woman's chart, it represents the type of man to whom she will be attracted. First-rate athletes often have a strong Mars in their charts and can be highly competitive to the point of aggressiveness.

Mars will demonstrate what you want for yourself and what your ambitions are. The sign it occupies will show how you will go about achieving your aims. For example, if your Mars is in the sign of Capricorn in your birth chart, you will direct your energies with prudence but in a serious and determined manner; these keywords are the characteristics of Capricorn.

If Mars is in your twelfth house, you will go to great lengths to conceal exactly where you expend your energy. This tendency to secrecy and strategic thinking is an attribute of the twelfth house.

JUPITER

benevolence, expansive energy, enthusiasm

Jupiter, the largest planet in our solar system was called the "Great Benefic" in medieval astrology. The God Jupiter was believed to be benevolent—doing good, being generous, and actively kind. Jupiter is thus concerned with enthusiasm in all aspects of life, promoting a positive attitude and great optimism. If Jupiter is your ruling planet (Sagittarius is ruled by Jupiter), you are one of the most fortunate of planetary types, particularly when it comes to any form of gambling, be it betting on a horse or dabbling in the stock market. You have a natural ability to do well and prosper, often by taking risks that others would avoid.

Thus, Jupiter is always associated with abundance. The word "expansive" sums up this planet's deepest quality. Everything associated with Jupiter is big—from embarking on epic journeys and adventures to undertaking massive projects. On a more spiritual level, Jupiter can indicate a strong desire to expand your higher consciousness, through an investigation of religion and philosophy. You will want to explore other cultures and learn from them, forever in search of higher ideals. This attitude, combined with your inborn generosity, explains why some of the world's greatest philanthropists have a strong Jupiter influence in their charts.

Jupiter will highlight your opportunities to expand in both your prosperity and personal growth areas. The sign it occupies in your chart will indicate how you will develop and expand. If, for example, Jupiter is in the sign of Virgo, you will do everything with an obsessive attention to detail, as this is a characteristic of Virgo.

The house placement of Jupiter in your birth chart will indicate where you can make the most of your enthusiasm in terms of advancement and expansion. If Jupiter is in your third house, then the emphasis falls on communication of all kinds, from writing to travel, as these are the attributes of the third house.

SATURN

wisdom, restriction, maturity

Saturn, the ringed planet, is the furthest planet from the Earth that can be seen with the naked eye. For this reason, Saturn is associated with limitations—completely the opposite of Jupiter, which is linked to expansion. Similarly, just as Jupiter was called the "Great Benefic," Saturn was known as the "Great Malefic," sometimes generally regarded as the bringer of gloom and doom. In marked contrast to the expansiveness of Jupiter, Saturn is conservative. Historically it was seen as the ruler of fate. Hence, the image of Saturn was traditionally shown with a scythe, the emblem of the grim reaper.

On the other hand, Saturn presided over the holiday feast of Saturnalia, during the period that we now call Christmas. At one time Saturn was thought to bring complications and handicaps into our lives. Nowadays, more positively, it is seen to elicit the traits of perseverance and tenacity, which can be used to overcome life's obstacles. For this reason, Saturn is often called "the teacher of the zodiac," or the "kick in the pants planet"—Saturn is planet that will get you off your butt and force you to grow. Its position in your chart will indicate where you are liable to meet your greatest confrontations and where you have the most to learn. A strongly placed Saturn endows you with a serious disposition. You will be self-reliant and practical, dependable but cautious. Saturn helps you to recognize your responsibilities in life and this understanding makes you "grow up." This explains Saturn's association with age, not so much in terms of advancing years but of maturity.

Saturn takes 28 years to move through the zodiac. Astrologers often talk about your "Saturn Return," which occurs after one full cycle through your chart. Your Saturn Return typically highlights a major change or reconsideration in your life. In truth, think of all the young 28-year-olds you know who are doing precisely that. It's a stage at which you start wondering, "Where is my life going?"

Saturn will show you what areas of life you need to address, particularly in the regions of responsibility and self-control. The sign that Saturn occupies in your birth chart will indicate how you will overcome the obstacles in your path and develop self-discipline. For example if Saturn is in the sign of Gemini, you will surmount your difficulties with adaptability and versatility, which are typical Gemini traits.

If Saturn is found in your second house, you will acquire financial skills only by facing up to the challenges that finances present. You will be considered highly astute because you will never commit yourself to a course of action until you have all the facts.

URANUS

psychic energy, innovation, change

Uranus takes about 84 years to traverse the whole zodiac and therefore, in a normal lifetime, spends about seven years in each sign. The planet was not discovered until 1781. This was a era of great new discoveries, new inventions, and change in the world. Uranus became associated with this transformation and has since been regarded as the planet of innovation and originality. If Uranus is strongly placed in your birth chart, you will almost certainly be unconventional and have some unusual ideas. Some people, however, may see you as simply eccentric, or as an out-and-out renegade. You will seek personal freedom by whatever means are available to you and, if necessary, you won't hesitate to rebel. You'll be ready to make changes wherever you think they are needed, and in implementing them may act impulsively. You will see nothing wrong with your behavior. You merely wish to help create a brave new world with a measure of freedom, understanding, and advances never known before. You long to be accepted for what you are: an original thinker who wishes to inspire change, rather than a crazy person who is intent on shocking other people.

Uranus represents the changes you wish to make in the world and the personal freedom you seek. Above all, Uranus is associated with your originality, in whatever way this is demonstrated. The position of Uranus in your chart will indicate *how* you will express your originality. As mentioned earlier, Uranus remains in each sign for seven years. Its influence will have the most effect on those who are born within that seven-year period when Uranus is in their Sun sign. If Uranus was in the sign of Aries when you were born, you will be headstrong, outspoken, and rather brusque in your approach, as these are Aries attributes.

The house in which Uranus is found in your birth chart will show where your Uranian attributes will manifest and in what areas your life-changes will take place. If Uranus is found in your eighth house, you will have an eventful life and will seek to achieve your objectives by replacing outworn ideas with new ones. This could come about via your interest in esoteric studies—possibly astrology.

NEPTUNE

calm, sensitivity, wisdom

Neptune, the planet associated with the God of the sea, rules our emotional imagination. It therefore affects those areas in your life in which you are most sensitive, imaginative, and idealistic. Because it takes this planet 165 years to circle the Sun, Neptune will remain in each sign for approximately 14 years. Its effect is therefore long-term, having a generational influence. This means that you, and everyone who is a peer born in your generation, will most likely experience the same Neptunian characteristics.

Neptune is related to dreams and fantasies. If Neptune occupies a strong position in your chart, this is where your dreams and fantasies will appear. Using your intuition and inspiration, you will crystallize your visions into ideals that transcend your everyday material life. Neptune creates a penetrating energy that seeps into the awareness in its own good time, in its own way. If you are unable to realize this potential within yourself, you will be forever discontented with your mundane existence. The difficulty comes in discovering how to use your latent strength, when you don't really know what it is. Your own particular path to idealism may take many forms. Some will find it through the arts such as painting, acting, poetry, or music, and some through healing, others through religion. Filmmakers and television producers often come under this Neptune influence. They are able to live in a fantasy world, making their own visions into reality and seeming to perform miracles—something definitely associated with Neptune. The fact that even actors who died many years ago still live on our TV screens is a very Neptunian concept. These people look real but they are no longer there . . .

If Neptune occupies a strong position in your chart you will have a certain almost mesmerizing charisma that others find hard to resist. This, linked with your creative imagination, will take you on a rewarding path.

The characteristics of Neptune are elusive, since it concerns the hidden side of you, your dreams and fantasies. Where there is Neptune in your chart, there will be unreality and obscurity as well as spirituality. The sign that Neptune occupies will show how you go about achieving your idealistic aims. If, for example, Neptune is in the sign of Cancer, you will exhibit great sensitivity, one of the chief Cancerian qualities.

The house where Neptune is found in your chart will show you where you will realize your dreams. If your Neptune is in the fifth house—the house of creative expression—you are likely to inspire others with your enthusiasm for one of the performing arts.

PLUTO

transformation, change

Pluto, the Roman god of the Underworld, is the outermost and slowest moving of the planets. "Underworld" does not refer to *hell*, as we might think, but to the *afterlife* of mythology, where souls underwent transformation. Pluto in your chart will mark the place where some kind of transformation occurs. Pluto takes over 247 years to go around the Sun, and it is possible that Pluto and its large nearby moon, Charon (pronounced Sharon), were both moons of Neptune that spun off when the solar system was in its early formation. The result is that Pluto has a far more wobbly orbit than the other planets, and this affects the time that it takes to move through the various signs. For instance, when Pluto travels through Scorpio, its orbit is as close to the Sun (perihelion) as it can get, so it takes 12 years to travel through the sign of Scorpio. Pluto takes 30 years to travel through Taurus, when it is furthest from the Sun (aphelion). Its average stay in any sign is 21 years. Pluto's long period of orbit makes its influence collective rather than personal, affecting all those born within the period that Pluto stays within the same sign. Again, like Neptune, it's influence is long-term and generational.

At its most profound level, Pluto is the planet of death and rebirth. However, in this case, death does not refer to the end of earthly life. It indicates the end of one thing, so that another newer thing can begin. The termination of one aspect of our life clears the way for something new. In this way, Pluto encourages you to overcome whatever obstacles hinder your progress in life, ensuring that you will eventually achieve your objectives. In some ways, Pluto actually compels change by upheaval. The difference between the transformation wrought by Pluto and the upheavals and revolutions brought by Uranus directly relates to the length of their orbits: in the case of Pluto (and its extremely long cycle), you probably know on some inner level that change is coming, whereas Uranus (with its much shorter orbit) can bring changes overnight. For instance, an unforeseen hurricane might make a large tree fall on to your house, necessitating a move away until the house is rebuilt (a Uranian event). On the other hand, a divorce upsets every part of your life (a Plutonic event), but it has most likely been in the cards for some time. It is also worth bearing in mind that change isn't necessarily a bad thing, but it always does take some adjusting to, even change that comes via a win in the lottery!

If Pluto occupies a strong position in your chart, you may be the person who initiates beneficial change, where others have not yet seen the need. In some cases, this desire for reformation can become so obsessive that others see you as simply wanting to destroy the status quo just for the sake of destruction. You may also be heavily into recycling, which is another Plutonic matter.

The three words that most clearly describe Pluto's effect are *elimination* and *illumination* through *transformation*.

If, for example, your Pluto is in the sign of Sagittarius (those born between 1995 and 2008), you will want to implement changes in time-honored principles through some form of philosophy or rebellion, which are Sagittarian characteristics. It is of interest here to note that parents and children will invariably never have Pluto in the same sign. This alone should give you some insight into the conflicts between parent and child!

If Pluto is in your first house, you will tend to implement change in an egotistical manner, since the first house is connected to the sense of self.

Finally...

Science is discovering more planets or planetoids within or far outside our solar system. One of these, Chiron, is used in astrology, and some astrologers use asteroids and many other features. In this book, we stick to the good old-fashioned planets and leave the rest to more advanced astrology students.

PISCES
ARIES
TAURUS
GEMINI
CANCER
LEO
VIRGO
LIBRA
SCORPIO
SAGITTARIUS
CAPRICORN
AQUARIUS

5

Your Rising Sign, or Ascendant

Your rising sign—also know as the ascendant—is determined by the exact hour of your birth, not just by day, month, and year. The rising sign indicates the starting point of a horoscope. It occupies the eastern horizon (dawn) at the time of your birth. The terms "rising sign" and "ascendant" are interchangeable; although to be precise, the ascendant is the exact degree of the sign that is rising. The ascendant (or rising sign) is found at the left hand side of the chart at the nine o'clock position. The ascendant is important in horoscopes because it describes the manner in which your personality is expressed. The ascendant also explains why two people with the same birthday can seem so different; because they are born at different hours, and even in different time zones, their personalities will express in quite distinct ways.

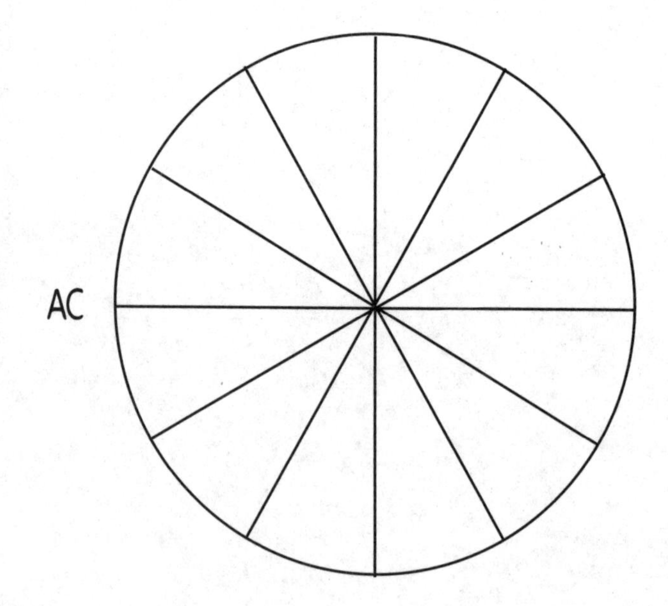

The details below explain a basic method for determining your rising sign:

1. The figure below shows the face of what appears to be a 24-hour clock. It is divided into 12 sections, each of which represents two hours.

2. Now draw on it the Sun symbol (a circle with a dot in the center) at the position that corresponds to the time of your birth. The example shows the position for someone who was born at approximately 3 a.m.

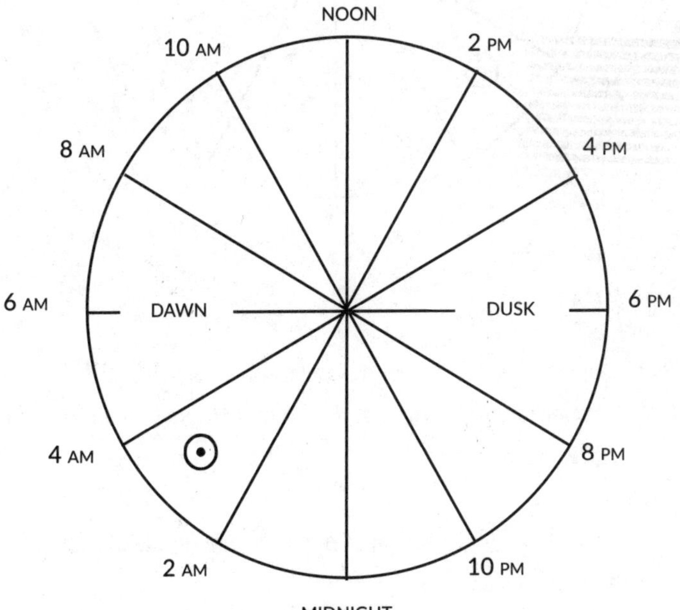

3. Draw the symbol for your birth sign on the line at the end of the section in which you have entered the Sun symbol. The example given is for someone born under the sign of Pisces.

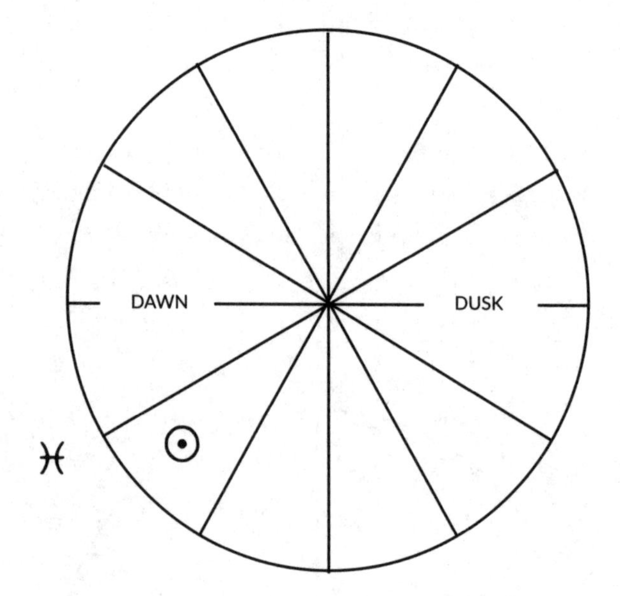

4. Draw the symbols for the other zodiac signs in the 2-hour intervals around the chart. Be careful to enter them in their correct order—that is, in an counter-clockwise direction.

5. The symbol that appears at 6 a.m. (dawn) on the clock face is your rising sign (AC).

You will now see that the rising sign for the person used in the example (having a Pisces Sun sign) is Aquarius.

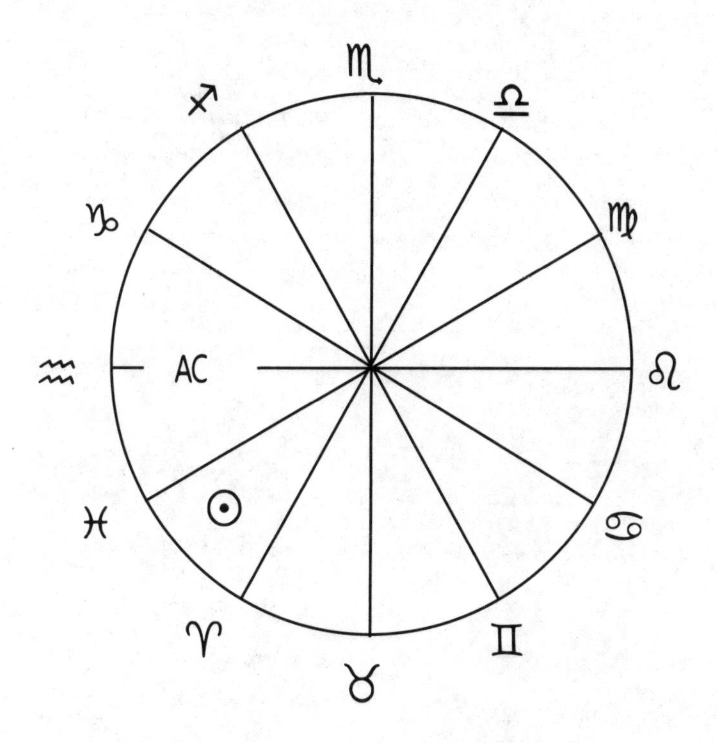

NOTE: If you are not yet confident about how to recognize and draw the Sun sign symbols on your "clock face," just write the names of the signs instead.

Rising Sign Characteristics

Ever met a Virgo who you could have sworn was really a Gemini? Confusingly, some people appear to be more like their rising sign than their Sun sign.

This is because your rising sign represents the face you show the world—it is your outward Self. Your Sun sign is who you are deep inside—and that's someone we don't often share with others, and often a Self we haven't yet discovered for ourselves.

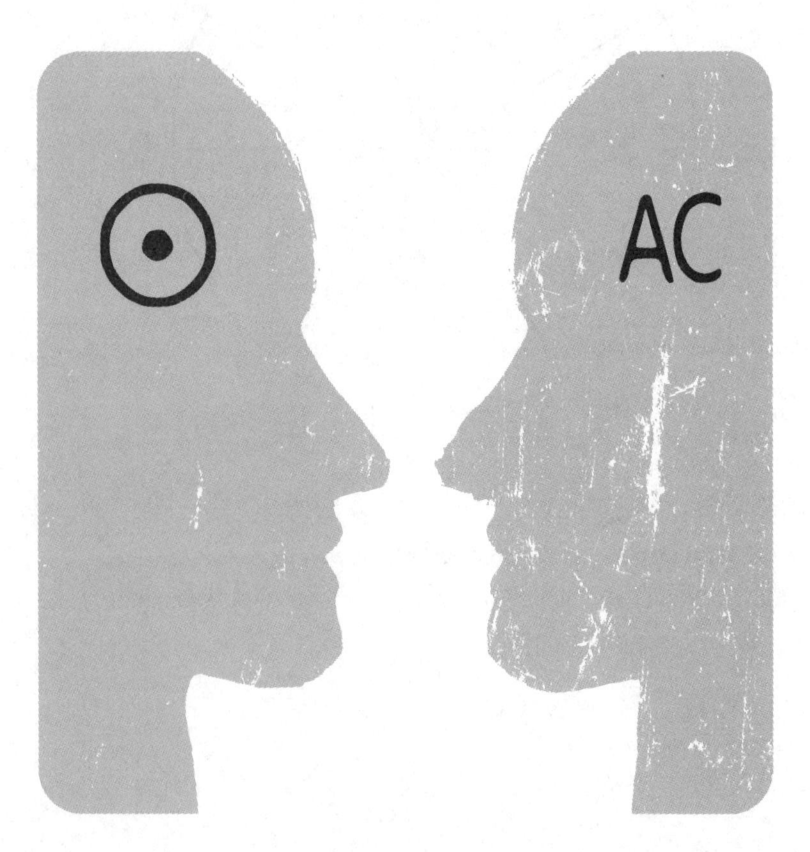

Most often, the rising sign will show the influences of our childhood. We tend to grow up "being" (or outwardly expressing) the person our parents treated us to be.

This section will give you an overview of what you can learn from your rising sign, and how it affects your overall makeup.

Aries Rising

If you have Aries rising, you're likely to be reserved and even slightly shy, which is probably due to a strict, though loving, childhood. However, this reservedness never holds you back from achievement. A career in an area that serves the public or in the armed forces will suit you well.

Taurus Rising

You are likely to be something of a materialist though you possess a lot of creative talent. Financial security is important to you, possibly because of childhood influences. You're a hard worker and completely reliable.

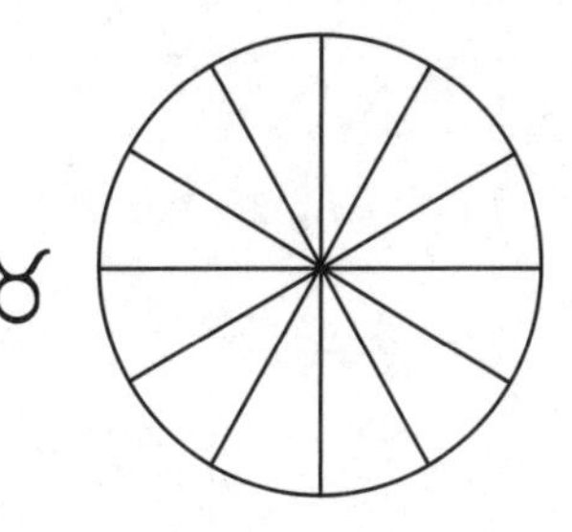

Gemini Rising

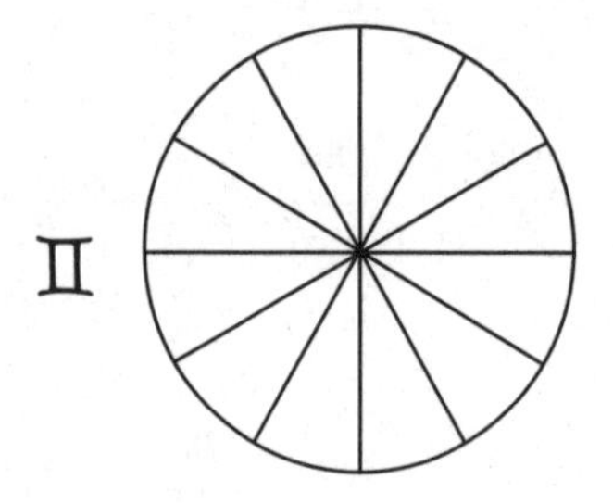

You're one of the talkers of the zodiac, though in childhood adults were probably too impatient to listen to you. As a result, you turn to friends and colleagues for support. Communication is certainly the name of the game for you, as far as a career is concerned.

Cancer Rising

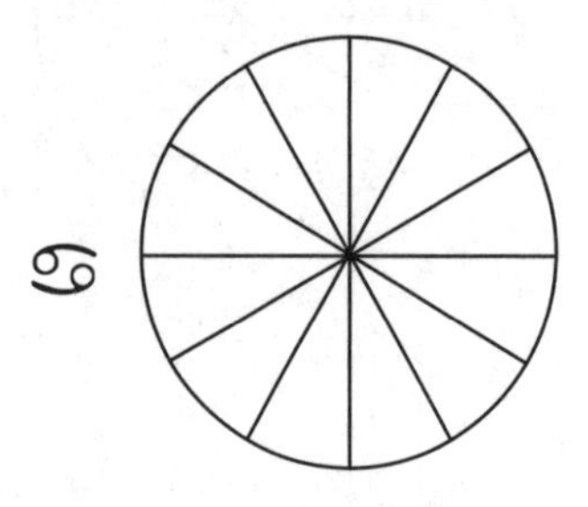

Your mother has probably been the strongest influence on your life and you are family oriented. In fact, your own parental instincts are strong and you are likely to be the "agony aunt," or confidant, to everybody you know. Even so, when it comes to business, you're a shrewd cookie.

Leo Rising

Your family undoubtedly expected a great deal from you. Their expectations could make you either conceited, or lacking in self-esteem. Either way, you work hard to succeed in all your undertakings because you love to be the center of attention.

Virgo Rising

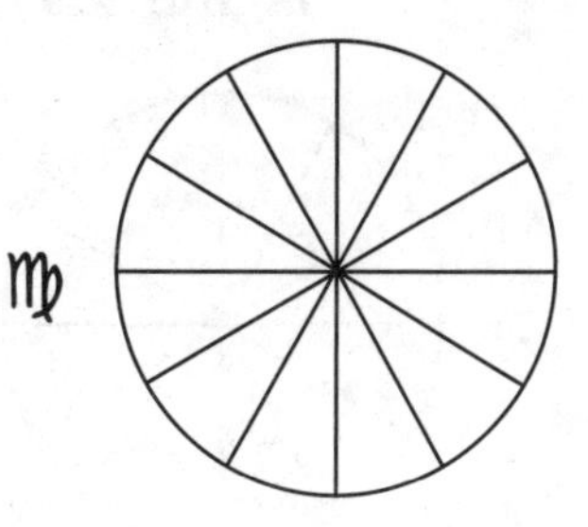

Being of service to others is likely to be your main aim in life, but you also do like to have your kindness appreciated. You're likely to be heavily involved with charitable organizations but always have time to love and support your family.

Libra Rising

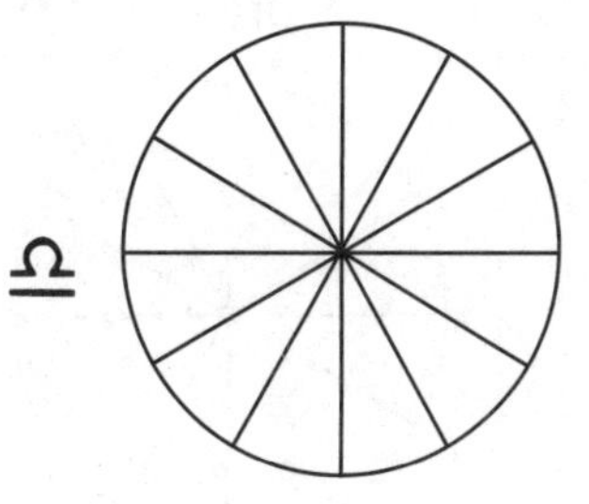

You're always able to see both points of view in an argument. This is a valuable attribute, but other people may sometimes regard you as indecisive. You have a most attractive personality and enjoy nothing more than bringing people together

Scorpio Rising

You tend to be secretive, probably due to childhood problems. This means you are likely to undertake confidential work of some kind. It's also important to you to work for the good of humanity.

Sagittarius Rising

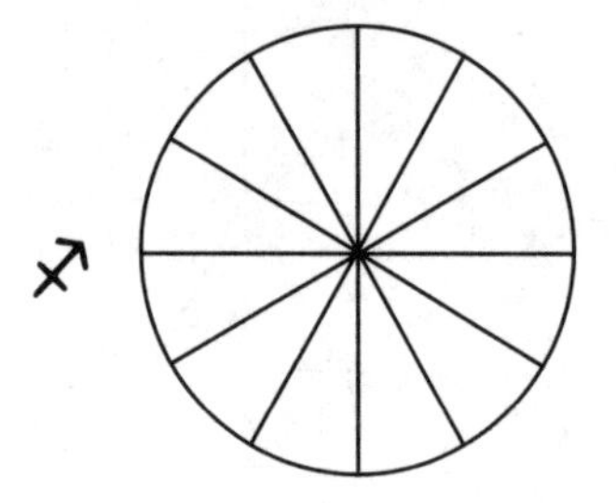

Freedom is essential to you, as is the companionship of other people. That being said, you're likely to take on a job that entails a fair amount of traveling. Emigration is a strong possibility for you, but you will make friends wherever you go.

Capricorn Rising

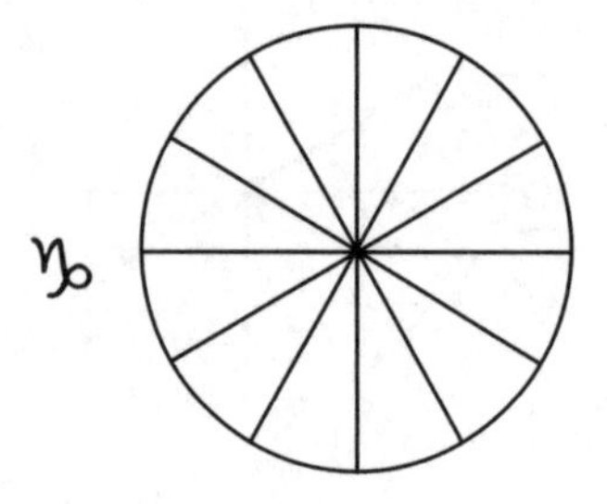

Events in your childhood taught you the importance of saving money, the value of hard work, and gave you a cautious attitude. You're ambitious, but overnight success is not for you. You're a plodder, climbing slowly and steadily toward your goal.

Aquarius Rising

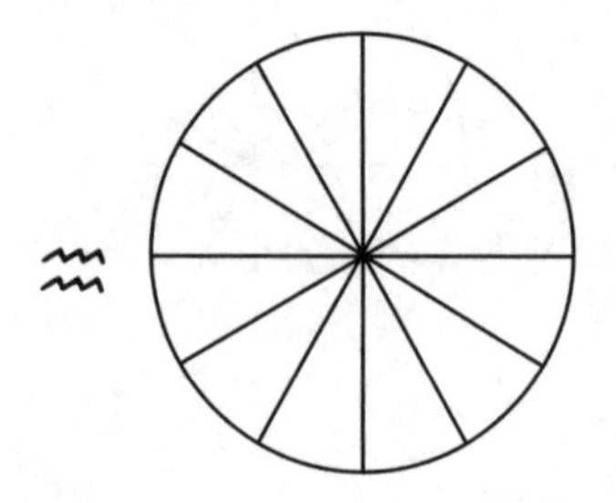

Anything that is new and unusual will appeal to you. This, in addition to your urge to help others, can lead you into a variety of humanitarian or ecological interests. You go your own way and don't readily accept advice.

Pisces Rising

Although you can be dreamy and impractical at times, childhood experiences have given you a lot of common sense. This, combined with your intuition, can make you highly successful in any job you undertake.

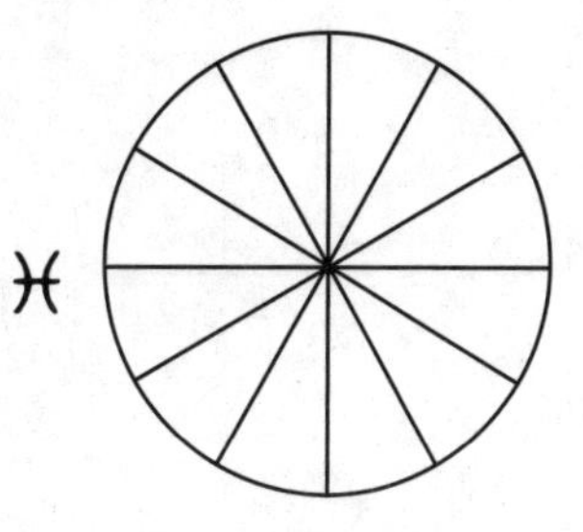

PISCES
ARIES
TAURUS
GEMINI
CANCER
LEO
VIRGO
LIBRA
SCORPIO
SAGITTARIUS
CAPRICORN
AQUARIUS

6 Moon Signs

The sign of the zodiac occupied by the Moon at the time of your birth is known as your Moon sign. Your Moon sign has a great influence on your life and your personality. This powerful effect is not surprising when we remember how strongly the lunar cycles affect the sea. The Moon represents your inner needs and feelings, your emotional responses, your habits, and the way you behave when sick, fatigued, or drunk. The Moon reveals what is hidden and private. It controls the unconscious/subconscious side of your personality, your true needs and attitudes rather than the polished face that you show the outside world. The Moon also reveals some information about your mother or other female figures in your life, their treatment of you, and the role models they might be.

Finding Your Moon Sign

We have included a quick and easy method here that works as a good rough guide for finding your Moon sign. It doesn't give the exact degree of the sign; therefore this system might be one sign off if your Moon was on a cusp when you were born, and this would be magnified if you were born around midnight. For complete accuracy and the exact degree of your Moon sign, you can try any of the following resources:

- Go to *www.astro.com* and find the Astrodienst service for a (currently) free birth chart.
- Check out Sasha Fenton's website (*www.sashafenton.com*) to see what suggestions are mentioned there.
- Visit an astrologer for personalized chart calculation and interpretation.

- Get further into astrology and consult an "ephemeris"—an encyclopedic book of tables for several centuries. A good online ephemeris can be found at *www.astro.com*
- Buy your own astrology software. You can obtain perfectly accurate software from various firms nowadays, costing not much more than you paid for this book. Check the Internet for such sources.

The Moonfinder Tables

- Start with Table 1 on page 84, which is titled "Moon on the First Day of the Month." Find your year of birth down the left-hand column, then track along to the month of your birth and find the sign that is listed there. Make a note of the sign.
- Now move to Table 2 on page 87, which is titled "Number of Signs to Add for Each Day of the Month." Find the day of your birth and check out the number to the right of that day in the "plus" column. Make a note of the number.
- Now move to Table 3 on page 87, which is titled "The Zodiac" and put your finger on the sign of the zodiac that you noted down in step one.
- Now count forward in a clockwise direction the number from the "plus" column that you noted down. The sign you end up at is your Moon sign.

Table 1: Moon on the First Day of the Month

	Jan	Feb	Mar	Apr	May	Jun	Jul	Aug	Sep	Oct	Nov	Dec
1925	Ari	Tau	Gem	Can	Leo	Lib	Sco	Sag	Aqu	Ari	Tau	Gem
1926	Leo	Vir	Lib	Sco	Sag	Aqu	Ari	Tau	Can	Leo	Vir	Lib
1927	Sag	Aqu	Aqu	Ari	Tau	Can	Leo	Vir	Sco	Sag	Cap	Pis
1928	Ari	Gem	Can	Vir	Lib	Sco	Sag	Aqu	Ari	Tau	Can	Leo
1929	Vir	Sco	Sco	Cap	Aqu	Pis	Ari	Gem	Leo	Vir	Sco	Sag
1930	Cap	Pis	Pis	Tau	Gem	Leo	Vir	Sco	Sag	Aqu	Pis	Ari
1931	Tau	Can	Can	Vir	Lib	Sag	Cap	Pis	Ari	Tau	Can	Leo
1932	Lib	Sag	Sag	Aqu	Pis	Tau	Gem	Can	Vir	Lib	Sag	Cap
1933	Pis	Ari	Tau	Gem	Can	Vir	Lib	Sag	Cap	Pis	Ari	Tau
1934	Can	Leo	Vir	Lib	Sag	Cap	Pis	Ari	Gem	Can	Leo	Vir
1935	Sco	Cap	Cap	Pis	Ari	Gem	Can	Leo	Lib	Sco	Cap	Aqu
1936	Ari	Tau	Gem	Leo	Vir	Lib	Sco	Cap	Pis	Ari	Gem	Can
1937	Leo	Lib	Lib	Sag	Cap	Aqu	Ari	Tau	Can	Leo	Lib	Sco
1938	Cap	Aqu	Aqu	Ari	Tau	Can	Leo	Lib	Sco	Cap	Aqu	Pis
1939	Tau	Gem	Can	Leo	Lib	Sco	Cap	Aqu	Ari	Tau	Gem	Leo
1940	Vir	Sco	Sag	Cap	Aqu	Ari	Tau	Can	Leo	Lib	Sco	Cap
1941	Aqu	Ari	Ari	Tau	Gem	Leo	Vir	Sco	Cap	Aqu	Ari	Tau
1942	Gem	Leo	Leo	Lib	Sco	Cap	Aqu	Ari	Tau	Gem	Leo	Vir
1943	Lib	Sag	Sag	Aqu	Pis	Tau	Gem	Leo	Vir	Lib	Sag	Cap
1944	Pis	Tau	Tau	Can	Leo	Lib	Sco	Sag	Aqu	Pis	Tau	Gem
1945	Leo	Lib	Lib	Sco	Cap	Aqu	Pis	Tau	Can	Leo	Vir	Lib
1946	Sag	Cap	Aqu	Pis	Tau	Gem	Leo	Vir	Sco	Sag	Cap	Aqu
1947	Ari	Gem	Gem	Leo	Vir	Sco	Sag	Cap	Pis	Ari	Gem	Can
1948	Vir	Lib	Sco	Cap	Aqu	Pis	Ari	Gem	Leo	Vir	Sco	Sag
1949	Cap	Pis	Pis	Tau	Gem	Leo	Vir	Sco	Sag	Cap	Pis	Ari
1950	Gem	Can	Can	Vir	Lib	Sag	Cap	Pis	Ari	Gem	Can	Leo
1951	Lib	Sag	Sag	Aqu	Pis	Ari	Gem	Can	Vir	Lib	Sco	Cap

Table 1: Moon on the First Day of the Month, cont.

	Jan	Feb	Mar	Apr	May	Jun	Jul	Aug	Sep	Oct	Nov	Dec
1952	Pis	Ari	Tau	Gem	Can	Vir	Lib	Sag	Cap	Pis	Ari	Gem
1953	Can	Vir	Vir	Vir	Lib	Sco	Sag	Aqu	Ari	Tau	Can	Leo
1954	Sco	Cap	Cap	Pis	Ari	Gem	Can	Vir	Lib	Sco	Cap	Aqu
1955	Ari	Tau	Gem	Can	Vir	Lib	Sco	Cap	Aqu	Pis	Tau	Gem
1956	Leo	Lib	Sco	Sag	Cap	Pis	Ari	Tau	Can	Leo	Lib	Sco
1957	Cap	Aqu	Pis	Ari	Tau	Can	Leo	Lib	Sag	Cap	Aqu	Pis
1958	Tau	Gem	Can	Leo	Lib	Sag	Cap	Aqu	Ari	Tau	Gem	Leo
1959	Vir	Sco	Sco	Cap	Aqu	Ari	Tau	Gem	Leo	Vir	Sco	Sag
1960	Aqu	Ari	Ari	Gem	Can	Leo	Vir	Sco	Cap	Aqu	Ari	Tau
1961	Can	Leo	Leo	Lib	Sco	Cap	Aqu	Ari	Gem	Can	Leo	Vir
1962	Sco	Sag	Sag	Aqu	Pis	Tau	Gem	Leo	Vir	Sco	Sag	Cap
1963	Pis	Tau	Tau	Can	Leo	Lib	Sco	Sag	Aqu	Pis	Tau	Gem
1964	Leo	Vir	Lib	Sco	Sag	Aqu	Pis	Tau	Can	Leo	Lib	Sco
1965	Sag	Aqu	Aqu	Ari	Tau	Gem	Leo	Lib	Sco	Sag	Aqu	Pis
1966	Ari	Gem	Gem	Leo	Vir	Sco	Sag	Aqu	Pis	Ari	Gem	Can
1967	Vir	Sco	Sco	Cap	Aqu	Pis	Ari	Gem	Can	Vir	Lib	Sag
1968	Cap	Pis	Ari	Tau	Gem	Leo	Vir	Sco	Sag	Aqu	Pis	Ari
1969	Gem	Can	Leo	Vir	Lib	Sag	Cap	Pis	Tau	Gem	Can	Leo
1970	Lib	Sco	Sag	Sco	Cap	Aqu	Pis	Tau	Can	Leo	Vir	Lib
1971	Aqu	Ari	Tau	Gem	Can	Vir	Lib	Sco	Cap	Aqu	Ari	Tau
1972	Ari	Vir	Vir	Sco	Sag	Cap	Pis	Ari	Gem	Can	Vir	Lib
1973	Sag	Cap	Cap	Pis	Ari	Gem	Can	Vir	Lib	Sag	Cap	Aqu
1974	Ari	Tau	Gem	Can	Vir	Lib	Sag	Cap	Pis	Ari	Tau	Gem
1975	Leo	Lib	Lib	Sag	Cap	Pis	Ari	Tau	Can	Leo	Lib	Sco
1976	Cap	Aqu	Pis	Ari	Tau	Can	Leo	Lib	Cap	Sag	Pis	Ari
1977	Tau	Can	Can	Vir	Lib	Sag	Cap	Pis	Ari	Tau	Can	Leo
1978	Vir	Sco	Sco	Cap	Aqu	Ari	Tau	Can	Leo	Vir	Sco	Sag

Table 1: Moon on the First Day of the Month, cont.

	Jan	Feb	Mar	Apr	May	Jun	Jul	Aug	Sep	Oct	Nov	Dec
1979	Aqu	Ari	Ari	Gem	Can	Leo	Vir	Sco	Sag	Aqu	Pis	Tau
1980	Gem	Leo	Vir	Lib	Sco	Cap	Aqu	Ari	Gem	Can	Leo	Vir
1981	Sco	Sag	Cap	Can	Pis	Tau	Gem	Leo	Lib	Sco	Sag	Cap
1982	Pis	Tau	Tau	Aqu	Leo	Lib	Sco	Sag	Aqu	Pis	Tau	Gem
1983	Leo	Vir	Lib	Sco	Sag	Aqu	Pis	Ari	Gem	Can	Vir	Lib
1984	Sag	Aqu	Aqu	Ari	Tau	Gem	Leo	Vir	Sco	Sag	Aqu	Pis
1985	Ari	Gem	Gem	Leo	Vir	Sco	Sag	Aqu	Pis	Ari	Gem	Can
1986	Vir	Lib	Sco	Cap	Aqu	Pis	Tau	Gem	Can	Vir	Lib	Sco
1987	Cap	Pis	Pis	Tau	Gem	Can	Vir	Lib	Sag	Cap	Pis	Ari
1988	Gem	Can	Leo	Vir	Lib	Sag	Cap	Pis	Tau	Gem	Leo	Vir
1989	Lib	Sag	Sag	Aqu	Pis	Tau	Gem	Leo	Vir	Lib	Sag	Cap
1990	Aqu	Ari	Ari	Gem	Can	Vir	Lib	Sag	Cap	Aqu	Ari	Tau
1991	Can	Vir	Vir	Sco	Sag	Cap	Aqu	Ari	Tau	Can	Vir	Lib
1992	Sco	Cap	Aqu	Pis	Ari	Gem	Can	Vir	Sco	Sag	Cap	Aqu
1993	Ari	Tau	Gem	Can	Vir	Lib	Sag	Cap	Pis	Ari	Tau	Gem
1994	Leo	Lib	Lib	Sag	Cap	Pis	Ari	Tau	Can	Leo	Lib	Sco
1995	Cap	Aqu	Pis	Ari	Tau	Can	Leo	Vir	Sco	Sag	Aqu	Pis
1996	Tau	Can	Can	Vir	Lib	Sco	Cap	Pis	Ari	Tau	Can	Leo
1997	Vir	Sco	Sco	Cap	Aqu	Ari	Tau	Can	Leo	Lib	Sco	Sag
1998	Aqu	Ari	Ari	Gem	Can	Leo	Lib	Sco	Sag	Aqu	Pis	Tau
1999	Gem	Leo	Leo	Lib	Sco	Sag	Aqu	Pis	Tau	Gem	Leo	Vir
2000	Sco	Sag	Cap	Aqu	Pis	Tau	Gem	Leo	Lib	Sco	Cap	Aqu
2001	Ari	Gem	Gem	Leo	Vir	Sco	Sag	Aqu	Pis	Ari	Gem	Can
2002	Vir	Lib	Sco	Sag	Aqu	Pis	Ari	Gem	Can	Leo	Lib	Sco
2003	Cap	Pis	Pis	Tau	Gem	Can	Leo	Lib	Sag	Cap	Pis	Ari
2004	Tau	Can	Leo	Vir	Lib	Sag	Cap	Pis	Tau	Gem	Can	Leo
2005	Lib	Sco	Sag	Cap	Pis	Ari	Gem	Can	Vir	Lib	Sco	Cap

Table 2: Number of Signs to Add for Each Day of the Month

Day	Plus	Day	Plus	Day	Plus
1	–	12	5	23	10
2	1	13	5	24	10
3	1	14	6	25	11
4	1	15	6	26	11
5	2	16	7	27	12
6	2	17	7	28	12
7	3	18	8	29	1
8	3	19	8	30	1
9	4	20	9	31	2
10	4	21	9		
11	5	22	10		

Table 3: The Zodiac

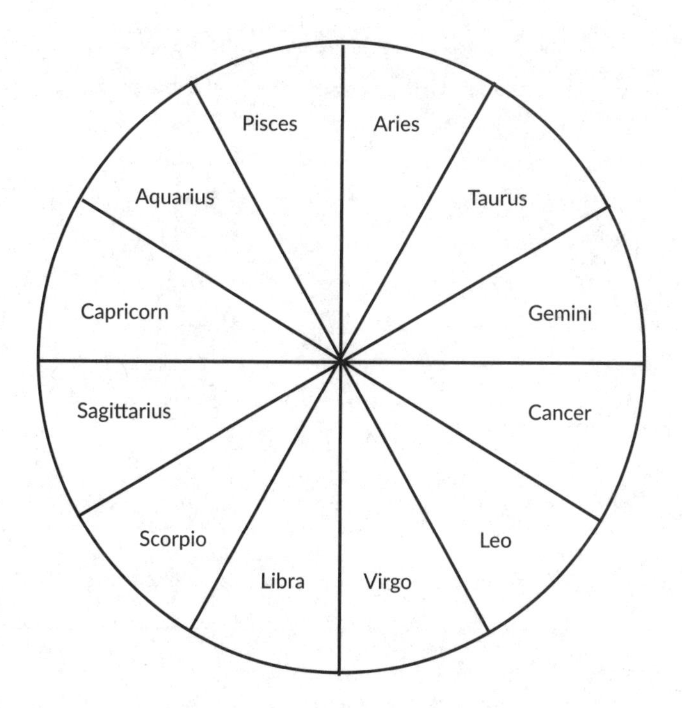

Example

Let us now experiment with Denzel Washington, who will be our example for the various interpretation sections throughout this book. Denzel's birth date is December 28, 1954.

- Denzel was born in 1954, so we find his year in the left-hand column of Table 1.
- We track along to the month of December and find that at the start of December, the Moon was in Aquarius.
- We look at Table 2 and find day number 28 (Denzel was born on the 28th).
- Beside his birthdate number, we find the number 12.
- Going now to Table 3, we start with the sign of Aquarius and count forward twelve signs, and it brings us back to Aquarius.

As we will see later in this book, Denzel's Moon is indeed in Aquarius.

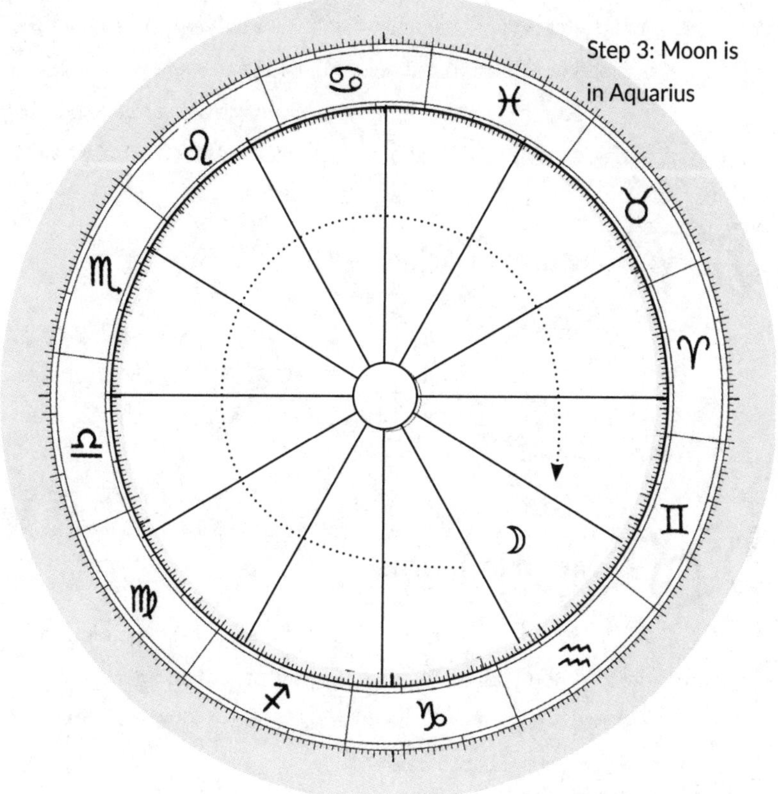
Step 3: Moon is in Aquarius
Step 2: Day 28—add 12
Step 1: December 1954—Moon is in Aquarius

Interpreting the Moon Sign

This book can offer only a very brief interpretation of how the Moon affects your character. If you want to know more about the fascinating side of your inner, emotional nature, read books such as *Your Secret Moon*, by Anne Christie, *How to Read Your Star Signs*, by Sasha Fenton, or *The Art of Chart Interpretation*, by Tracy Marks.

☽♈ Moon in Aries

Speed could be your middle name: you are quick to react, quick to think, quick to speak, and unfortunately quick-tempered. You are restless, impatient, and excitable, preferring to take charge of any situation rather than to assist.

☽♉ Moon in Taurus

You take your time reaching decisions and never rush into anything. When you finally make up your mind, you are determined and persistent. Security and material possessions are necessary to your emotional happiness.

☽♊ Moon in Gemini

You're a naturally intense person, but not too eager to form emotional ties. You make an excellent student, but have a tendency to discard your latest great idea in favor of an exciting new project.

☽♋ Moon in Cancer

Because you are sensitive and intuitive, you can sometimes be somewhat moody and withdrawn. You enjoy your home, and a happy family life is important to your emotional well-being.

☽♌ Moon in Leo

You are highly ambitious but always cheerful and warm-hearted. Emotionally you are inclined to be rather over-sentimental. Your organizing ability gives you the self-confidence needed for dealing with the public.

☽♍ Moon in Virgo

You tend to be shy and retiring, but you shine when it comes to dealing with business details. Always methodical, neat and clean, you are keenly interested in hygiene and health. Try not to be too critical of yourself or others.

☽♎ Moon in Libra

Your greatest need is for harmony. It is essential to your well-being that you find affable friends and partners. Fortunately, your personal charm means that you will have no difficulty in attracting the right sort of person to fulfill these requirements.

☽♏ Moon in Scorpio

You are emotionally highly charged, with intense feelings about virtually everything. However, you tend to hide your true feelings, usually as a result of being deeply hurt at some time. You enjoy the company of the opposite sex, but occasionally let your sensuality run away with you.

☽♐ Moon in Sagittarius

Freedom is almost an obsession with you, so much so that you are always restless and eager to "get away from it all." This applies physically and mentally. You're quite likely to suddenly quit your job, your home, or your partner and take off in search of new pastures.

☽♑ Moon in Capricorn

You are reserved by nature and need to find emotional security through a happy home and material possessions. You have outstanding managerial abilities together with ambition and the capacity for hard work. These traits should see you in a high executive position.

☽♒ Moon in Aquarius

You are strongly independent by nature. This makes you wary of having your personal freedom threatened by outsiders. As a result, you avoid becoming 100 percent emotionally involved until you are entirely sure of your ground.

☽♓ Moon in Pisces

You're easy-going and super-sensitive to the needs of others. You may even have psychic abilities. Don't allow your lack of confidence to discourage you from making the most of your artistic talents.

PISCES
ARIES
TAURUS
GEMINI
CANCER
LEO
VIRGO
LIBRA
SCORPIO
SAGITTARIUS
CAPRICORN
AQUARIUS

7
Houses of the Zodiac

When a birth chart is constructed, the ascendant is placed on the left-hand side, at a "9 o'clock" position. The chart is divided from this point into twelve parts of 30 degrees each (remember, there are 360 degrees in a circle). These parts are numbered counterclockwise from 1 to 12.

These twelve divisions are known as the "houses of the zodiac" or the "astrological houses." They are the same for every chart, with the first house starting from the first degree of the ascendant. The houses themselves do not have names; they are referred to simply by their number. Each of the first six houses (1 through 6) relate to you personally as an individual. The last six houses (7 through 12) are associated with your attitude toward others.

The houses never move; only the planets and signs move around the zodiac. As such, it is more than likely that a zodiac sign can spread across two houses. The lines that mark the divisions between the houses are called the house cusps. Even if the majority of the house is in a different sign from the cusp, the sign that the cusp occupies must not be ignored, because it is important.

Regardless of the movement of the zodiac through the houses, each house has a "natural" association with both a sign of the zodiac and a planet. These correspondences are listed in the table on page 97. The reason this natural placement is important is that it relates to what astrologers call "weak" and "strong" placements. The natural sign for the first house is Aries. If you are an Aries, and Aries was passing through the first house at the time of your birth, then this is a strong placement for you.

Each house relates to a specific department of human life and indicates in which area the energies of the signs and will operate. The planets represent what the energy is, the signs represent how that energy will be used, and the house represents where that energy will manifest.

House	Sign	Planet
First	Aries	Mars
Second	Taurus	Venus
Third	Gemini	Mercury
Fourth	Cancer	Moon
Fifth	Leo	Sun
Sixth	Virgo	Mercury
Seventh	Libra	Venus
Eighth	Scorpio	Pluto
Ninth	Sagittarius	Jupiter
Tenth	Capricorn	Saturn
Eleventh	Aquarius	Uranus
Twelfth	Pisces	Neptune

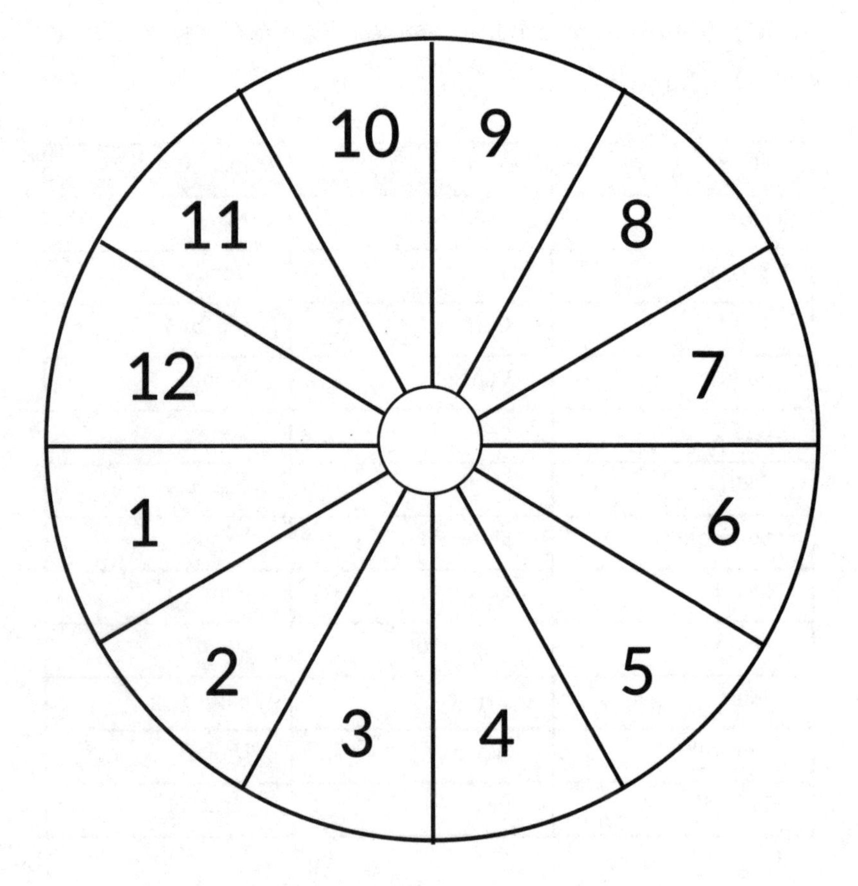
10
9
11
8
12
7
1
6
2
5
3
4

First House

This is the most important house of the zodiac, since it is here that your ascendant is found. Your first house indicates your outward personality, your ego, and your physical and mental health. Your physical appearance will also be revealed here, the attributes depending on the sign on the cusp of this house. The first house also has a bearing on how you will act and react toward others. Any planet that is found in the first house will have an especially strong influence on your character. As we have mentioned in the section on Rising Sign, the planet found nearest the cusp (edge) of the first house is known as your rising sign or ascendant, and will have an especially powerful effect on you.

Second House

The second house represents whatever you hold dear in life. It covers financial affairs, your possessions, and your personal resources. Your capacity for earning, the accumulation of worldly goods, and how you spend your money are also represented here. Your thinking in this sector will tend to be more about tangibles than about principles or theories. At a deeper level, the second house relates to your attitude toward your partner—do you see your partner as a possession? Do you need emotional safety as much as financial security? The answers to these questions will be shown by the sign on the cusp of this house and any planets it contains.

Third House

This house is associated with your immediate environment and the way you communicate within it. Thus, the third house is concerned with your day-to-day contacts—family members such as siblings, grandparents, aunts, uncles, and cousins (but not parents), your casual acquaintances, and your neighbors and friends. The third house is also associated with your attitude toward these relationships and your need to communicate with the people involved. Thus it covers all forms of correspondence as well as personal contact. It also covers short journeys—to visit and communicate with your contacts—and self-expression.

Fourth House

The fourth house represents your home as your private base. It also represents your parents and any property that you may own. You may imagine the fourth house as being the womb. Here there is security, protection, your physical base, privacy, and a strong connection with your mother. Allied to this are the circumstances in which you grew up and your reaction to childhood experiences. Here is your inner world and what is hidden from others.

Fifth House

The fifth house deals with creative expression and the recreational aspects of your life. It has much to do with your relationship with your children and with your father. On the recreational side, the fifth house is connected to the pleasure you take in games, gambling (including financial speculation), and the performing arts. Sports, too, are connected with this house, especially risky ventures such as skydiving, bungee jumping, and white-water rafting. Leisure and holidays are represented by the fifth house, as are your attitudes toward your teachers, colleagues, advisors, and guru. This house doesn't concern open, marriage-type relationships, or even a long-term affair in which money, business, goods, and resources are shared; this house relates to the fun type of love affair that exists only for itself.

Sixth House

This house covers health matters, your career, and your service to others. It concerns your health, hygiene, and general well-being, especially as regards your bodily functions. Connected with these, and included here, are your diet and the exercise you do to maintain good health. Your health may also be affected by your habits, which are also associated with the sixth house. Any planets in this house will indicate where you may encounter problems or find opportunities in your working relationships This is also the house of self analysis; you will examine your obligations and attitude toward your partner, employees, employer, colleagues, and subordinates through your daily work.

Seventh House

The seventh house is all about one-on-one relationships; it concerns the kind of partner you are likely to attract. The seventh house covers your associations on all emotional and professional levels, including your attitude toward your children. The sign on the cusp of the seventh house will give some indication of your emotional makeup as it relates to both your personal and your business life. This includes your attitude toward marriage and your potential rapport with any business partners. The seventh house also governs contracts, agreements, and covenants. Any planets in this house will give some indication of what type of partnership is going to be important to you. Bear in mind that the first house, which is opposite the seventh, is all about you; this house is about relating to others. This house will also reveal the qualities that you refuse to accept in yourself and yet project onto others.

Eighth House

Just as the second house is concerned with your money and possessions, the eighth house, which is opposite the second, is about how you deal with money gained from others by legacies or bequests. It also involves fiscal issues that are outside your control, such as taxes and banks. This house concerns your financial abilities and the way that you deal with money shared with your partner or anyone else closely connected to you. The eighth house is very much concerned with your deepest emotions, your anxieties and traumas, as well as your (usually hidden) bedroom emotions—your attitude toward sexual intimacy. It can show the kind of sexual preferences that you have; for example, the eighth house in Taurus or Libra would show you to be attracted by good looks. The eighth house in Sagittarius might make foreigners or those who have a great sense of humor irresistible to you. On a deeper level, this house is associated with your attitude toward the cycle of birth, life, death, and the afterlife.

Ninth House

If distant lands and foreign cultures attract you, then you probably have some strong placements in your ninth house. While the third house was about your immediate environment, the ninth house, opposite the third, is about expansion through travel and wider experience. Higher education of any kind, but particularly philosophy, law, or religion, is associated with this house. This could lead to your spiritual expansion and thence to the development of any psychic abilities that you may potentially have. It is all about learning who you really are, the meaning of life, and the development of your ideals. The ninth house concerns profound mental states and is connected with publishing, literature, and the law. It is also about the dream state and, through your dreams, is connected with prophecy and foresight.

Tenth House

While the fourth house was about your private life, the tenth house concerns your outer life—status and position in life. It may relate to your career, but it could equally concern your social standing, wealth, or class. It shows how you strive to establish yourself in the community and how the world views your position. The sign on the cusp of this house will indicate your aspirations and the vocation you are liable to pursue in order to reach your goal. This far-reaching connection is associated with your professional achievement and its bearing on your social responsibilities. Here your personal aims and ambitions are highlighted, plus the effects that parental expectations have had on them. However, just as the tenth house is about your achievements in the public domain, it also concerns any scandal or public disgrace that may befall you.

Eleventh House

This is the house of friendships and group activities and is related to your need for social and intellectual security. The relationships you form here will be strictly platonic, made on an idealistic, intellectual basis. From this will spring your search for your own social conscience and life objectives. These ideals will reflect your hopes and wishes for the future, not only for yourself but also for the benefit of the community as a whole. The eleventh house also highlights your need for a secure social life, and the way in which you will work with other people. Your original, innovative ideas will lead you to identify with an organization rather than with any one individual. Cynics might call this the "let's all get together and save the whale" house, but it can just as easily relate to the group you meet every Saturday night for gossip and a night out on the town.

Twelfth House

The twelfth house covers all that is hard to understand and therefore difficult to explain. Within the twelfth house is every one of those secrets that you carry with you throughout your life (consciously or subconsciously), the secrets that you never reveal—and which may be at the root of any psychological problems. This is the house of mystery, and you may be drawn to conspiracies, intrigues, and romantic liaisons. It is linked to prisons, hospitals, and institutions of all kinds. The need for solitude and deep contemplation is stressed, and there is also a danger of self-deception. This is sometimes seen as a house of limitation, and some kind of sacrifice may be indicated. Only by facing restrictions experienced, and seeking to understand their cause, can the individual learn to deal with them.

This house has some peculiar connections. For instance, many politicians have planets here, as it seems to represent the strategist who can plan things in his head or with an inner circle, and then make them happen. It also has connections with music and art, although these activities might be part the need to escape that this house represents.

House	Keywords for interpretation
1	outward personality, ego
2	emotional security, what you hold dear
3	communication, day-to-day contacts
4	home, parents, property
5	creative expression, recreation
6	health, general well-being
7	relationships, partners, children
8	personal finances, possessions
9	mental expansion, travel, higher education
10	status, position in life, career
11	social consciousness, ideals, intellect
12	subconscious, secrets, occult

PISCES
ARIES
TAURUS
GEMINI
CANCER
LEO
VIRGO
LIBRA
SCORPIO
SAGITTARIUS
CAPRICORN
AQUARIUS

The Aspects

8

"Aspect" is the term used for the angular relationship between the planets, as positioned on a birth chart. Each planet exerts an influence on the other planets. Whether the planets are adjacent or opposite, near or far, the energy of one planet will affect the energy of another—the influence can be weak or strong, harmonious or conflicting. The aspect that two planets make to each other is a matter of geometry: within the 360 degrees of the birth chart, the distance between planets is measured by degree.

The following describes the most important aspects:

☌ Conjunction

Planets are in conjunction (close) when they are within 10 degrees of each other. A conjunction is usually a harmonious aspect because the planets that form a conjunction are energies that are blended. Sun conjunct Mercury blends the energies of each together. However, it is possible that conjunction might also be difficult depending on the planets that are involved—Pluto conjunct Saturn can indicate a massive life challenge.

Sextile

Planets are two signs apart ,or around 60 degrees apart. This is a harmonious aspect. It symbolizes the potential to make connections, and indicates natural attunement and skill.

Square

Planets are three signs or around 90 degrees apart. This is usually an inharmonious aspect since it involves planets with divergent energies. A square aspect usually indicates that energy must be expended—something needs to be torn down so that something new can be built.

Trine

Planets are four signs or 120 degrees apart. This is a harmonious aspect and indicates balance among the planets' energies; these planets generally complement one another.

Opposition

Planets are six signs or 180 degrees apart, therefore, opposite each other. This is often thought of as an inharmonious aspect because the planets are "opposing" each other. But in truth, an opposition often represents opportunity—two opposing planets create tension, but sometimes this tension can have positive results.

There are many lesser aspects, but these are the main ones, and that is plenty for a beginner to consider.

When inspecting a chart it should be noted that a certain tolerance or leeway is allowed in the accuracy of the angles measured. This is known as the *orb of influence* and this varies according to the aspect.

These orbs of influence are as follows:

for a conjunction—10 degrees

for a sextile—6 degrees

for a square—6 degrees

for a trine—6 degrees

for an opposition—8 degrees

To sum up:

- **Harmonious aspects**: Trines and sextiles are harmonious, soft, or easy aspects that usually have a beneficial effect.

- **Inharmonious aspects:** Squares and oppositions are the inharmonious, dynamic, or hard aspects that may present difficulties, but should be seen in a positive manner as challenges.

- Conjunctions are often fortunate or difficult depending upon the energy of the planets that are involved.

ASPECTS OF THE SUN

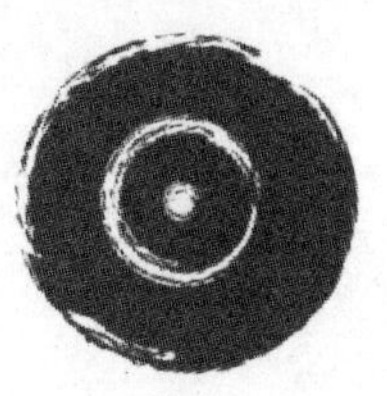

Planets aspected by the Sun will always be important in a chart, as they will contribute in no small manner to your life and character.

Sun to Moon

Harmonious aspects

You are a balanced and well-adjusted personality who will enjoy a highly successful relationship with your family, friends, and partner. You are equally at home with members of either sex. Harmony in your emotional life and success in all your business activities is indicated. A highly creative person with a wealth of ideas is usually found here.

Inharmonious aspects

Any aspects here will emphasize your Sun sign attributes. You may encounter emotional complications that lead to frustration and restlessness. Your challenge here is to avoid stress. You need to focus on being objective and avoiding extreme mood swings.

Sun to Mercury

Mercury is the closest planet to the Sun, and as such, it's position in the birth chart can never be more than 28 degrees away from the Sun. Therefore, only the conjunction is possible. If you have Sun conjunct Mercury you will almost certainly be strong-willed, with a high intellect. You may find that you are unable to form unbiased opinions, as all your judgments tend to be subjective. This is compounded by the fact that you hate to admit that you are in the wrong and you may find it difficult to change your mind.

Sun to Venus

Another planet whose orbit is close to the Sun. Since the Sun can never be more than 48 degrees from Venus in the birth chart, the only strong aspect will be the conjunction. If your Sun is conjunct Venus you will possess all the charm that is usually associated with this planet. You will be optimistic, friendly, and have a charismatic personality. Although others are unaware of it, your nature is influenced by the fact that you have a desperate need to be loved. You may show some creative, artistic, or musical talent.

Sun to Mars

Harmonious aspects

Although these aspects are soft and beneficial, the influence of Mars means that they will always be challenging. However, you enjoy a challenge, in all its competitive aspects, whether it is in sports, your emotional life, or in business. You always feel that you are up to this challenge, ready to take on more than your share of the work that is involved and see it through to completion.

Inharmonious aspects

Here the influence of Mars will make you more insistent and forceful. Your challenge here is to avoid appearing stubborn and tactless.

Sun to Jupiter

Harmonious aspects

"Easy" is the appropriate word here. You'll do anything for the easy life and motivate yourself only when you can see no means of escape. This is exactly the attitude to be expected from someone who is as optimistic as you are. You are serious about life and the direction that you wish to take, but this somber façade is balanced by a good sense of humor.

Inharmonious aspects

Here your easy-going nature may be carried to excess, to the point where you tend to be smug and self-satisfied. Your challenge here is to rise above this and apply your innate good business sense.

Sun to Saturn

Harmonious aspects

Saturn will stabilize your emotions and lead you to form friendships with those who are older than you are. Although you are competent in all that you do, you move steadily and your watchword through life is "caution," since you prefer to remain in the background. However, you don't allow this prudence to stand in the way of your ambition to succeed. You will receive support from others.

Inharmonious aspects

The danger here is that you may be so over-cautious that you become inhibited, and then you achieve nothing. Your challenge here is to overcome these limitations.

Sun to Uranus

Harmonious aspects

Uranus softly aspecting the Sun indicates a life of diversity and change. You will be forever seeking new experiences and—metaphorically—new mountains to climb because you enjoy the challenge. You are by nature a good teacher who delights in sharing knowledge with others in a logical and easily understood manner.

Inharmonious aspects

You are capable of strong self-expression but your challenge here is to avoid revealing your rebelliousness. Additionally, you should guard against making drastic changes in the heat of the moment.

Sun to Neptune

Harmonious aspects

You are one of the fortunate people who never opens your mouth and puts your foot in it. You have an extremely sensitive nature, which may make you somewhat impractical. To compensate, you will show strong artistic ability and are conscious of your own talent in this direction. You find it difficult to cope with rejection and any form of criticism wounds you deeply.

Inharmonious aspects

Your tendency to undervalue yourself can lead to dishonesty or evasion as a means of escape from your problems. Your challenge here is to avoid this trap.

Sun to Pluto

Harmonious aspects

With the Sun in easy aspect to Pluto, everything you do you will involve great intensity and honesty. You don't suffer fools gladly. You are confident that you can achieve anything you want and, if you do encounter setbacks, you will bounce back quickly. Your natural talents will enable you to excel at any task, occupation, or profession that you decide is the one for you. However, something in your background lingers and leaves you full of some kind of underlying resentment. You may suffer love/hate relationships with family members.

Inharmonious aspects

Your obsessive nature can become such that other people find you difficult to deal with. Your challenge here is to be aware of this trait and compensate for it by being less stubborn. Resentment and hidden hurt from the past never really leave you.

Sun to Ascendant

Harmonious aspects

Harmony and balance are essential to you. You are also very sure of yourself and you know what is right for you. This self-confidence can irritate your superiors. Quite rightly, they fear for their own positions when you keep coming up with such original ideas. You aim for the top simply because you cannot bear the idea of being subservient to others less talented than you are.

Your kind-hearted and selfless nature ensures that all your friendships and partnerships will flourish and prosper.

Inharmonious aspects

Guard against giving the impression of insincerity in your dealings. You hate criticism and your challenge here is to learn how to cope with it.

ASPECTS OF THE MOON

Lunar aspects affect your inner nature and your feelings.

Moon to Mercury

Harmonious aspects

If your Moon is well aspected to Mercury, you are sure to be endowed with more than the average amount of common sense. Success comes through using your practical creative talents. Your perfect partner will be someone who is your intellectual equal and who is equally goal oriented. You're a great one for networking and this will result in many social contacts. You are not one to stand aside and allow others to make decisions for you.

Inharmonious aspects

Practical you may be, but on the emotional level, you have much to learn. Your challenge is not to allow your heart to rule your head.

Moon to Venus

Harmonious aspects

Your friendly and affectionate nature ensures your popularity with both sexes. You're considerate and kindly, the sort of person that others seek when they need a shoulder to cry on. You are quite capable of handling your finances and do not like it when someone else tries to interfere. You feel that you have arranged an uncomplicated life for yourself and strongly object to outside intervention.

Inharmonious aspects

Your difficulty in expressing your true feelings may result in some unhappy experiences regarding a love affair. Your challenge is to discriminate between true friends and sycophants.

Moon to Mars

Harmonious aspects

Easy aspects between Moon and Mars indicate that you are blessed with good health. Friends regard you as a good judge of character and often ask your opinion on partnership issues. You tend to react to others subjectively and always give them the benefit of the doubt—you are not prone to jumping to conclusions. You tend to be emotionally vulnerable.

Inharmonious aspects

Worry can drain your energies and, because you let your emotions run away with you, your health suffers. Your challenge here is to develop more self-control and avoid quarrels.

Moon to Jupiter

Harmonious aspects

With these aspects, you will almost certainly be endowed with superior judgment, integrity, and honesty. You are a likeable character who will be popular with your many friends. This is partly because, without incontrovertible proof, you will never see the evil in others. On the contrary, you find the potential for honorable qualities in everyone and react as though these were their natural characteristics.

Inharmonious aspects

You tend to be extravagant and careless with money, and the challenge here is to exercise more self-control. If you find this difficult, allow someone else to take charge of your finances.

Moon to Saturn

Harmonious aspects

You have a very practical outlook with a mature sense of responsibility. Always ready to listen to another's viewpoint, you never jump to conclusions. Indeed, you prefer to discuss problems openly in order to reach a solution acceptable to all. A personal relationship will be acceptable to you only if your partner is willing to share your desire for success.

Inharmonious aspects

You lack self-confidence and tend to bottle up your emotions, suffering from anxiety or depression as a result. Your challenge here is to adopt a more balanced attitude where you can live and let live.

Moon to Uranus

Harmonious aspects

You are a determined person with strong ideals. You will strive for success against all odds, though you will always work at your own pace, shunning those who try to hurry you along. Your emotional make-up is such that your choice of partner will be logical, rather than romantic.

Inharmonious aspects

You are never willing to let go of your ideals and other people often regard you as being stubborn. You often go to extremes to get your own way. The challenge here is to channel your energies into being more cooperative and less obstructive.

Moon to Neptune

Harmonious aspects

Both the Moon and Neptune are linked to the emotions, and this aspect may overload you with sentiment. You will be emotionally sensitive and have a vivid imagination. You're so much involved with so many projects, both social and personal, that you are in danger of damaging your health. Make a habit of getting away from time to time, to recharge your batteries. It is essential to your well-being that you should have time to yourself.

Inharmonious aspects

Your strong emotions sometimes get the better of you and your health suffers as a result. Your challenge here is to be more rational and objective, avoiding your escapist tendencies.

Moon to Pluto

Harmonious aspects

When change becomes inevitable, you'll find it relatively easy to make the necessary adjustments to your life. You won't even have to think about them—they'll be instinctive responses. You empathize strongly with young people and enjoy their company. They feel that you understand them and their problems, and they respond by taking you into their confidence.

Inharmonious aspects

You hate change of any kind, particularly change to your lifestyle. Even the thought of having to make alterations can upset you. Your challenge is to accept the inevitable with good grace.

Moon to Ascendant

Harmonious aspects

These aspects herald a happy home life that is colored by your infectious good humor. You find that you have useful talents and are able to put them to good use. You are quite philosophical and are interested in trying to understand what makes you (and other people) tick. In your youth, criticism really upsets you but, as you get older, you are less vulnerable.

Inharmonious aspects

Your difficulty in expressing your emotions is at odds with maintaining any close personal relationship. Your challenge is to find positive ways in which you can build up your self-confidence.

ASPECTS OF MERCURY

Mercury rules the mental functioning, education, communication, siblings, neighbors, short journeys, commuting, magic, and thieves.

Mercury to Venus

Harmonious aspects

The gentle aspect of Mercury with Venus endows you with a tender, agreeable disposition. Others will be charmed by your warm and friendly nature, though they know you are no pushover. They respect your views, which are particularly well expressed in any form of debate. Your communicative ability is not only verbal; you may also be a skillful writer, always able to express yourself clearly.

Inharmonious aspects

Because Mercury and Venus are never more than 76 degrees apart, there are no inharmonious aspects.

Mercury to Mars

Harmonious aspects

You possess a great deal of common sense, honesty, and imagination. These traits are fed by your insatiable curiosity; you are never afraid to ask questions. You are fair and just but you will not suffer fools gladly. Your truthfulness is plain for all to see—and sometimes you're too candid for your own good.

Inharmonious aspects

You have a tremendous amount of energy and sometimes find that energy difficult to control. Your challenge is to find ways in which you can channel your energies constructively and effectively to the advantage of yourself and others.

Mercury to Jupiter

Harmonious aspects

Your organizational abilities and your flair for words combine with your good sense of humor to make you a natural and popular leader. You are mentally a live wire, leaving others reeling as you drive ever onwards. You're extremely shrewd and nobody can fool you. Once they've encountered your rapier-like tongue they don't try again.

Inharmonious aspects

You have a tendency here to be over-optimistic and for this reason, you are prone to exaggeration. Analytical opinion is not one of your strengths. Your challenge here is to develop a more constructive approach to life.

Mercury to Saturn

Harmonious aspects

You're a highly ambitious person, and you will work long and hard to achieve your goals. This characteristic can make your friends regard you as too serious, but they learn differently as they get to know you better. Your studious nature does mean that you tend to lead a solitary life; you're certainly not a social butterfly. Your studies involve a lot of writing and yet you may relax by writing for pleasure.

Inharmonious aspects

You expect too much of yourself and tend to withdraw from society if you don't achieve your ambitions. Your challenge is to learn to be more tolerant of people who don't understand you.

Mercury to Uranus

Harmonious aspects

Your main interest will be in original and unusual subjects that you pursue with an enquiring mind. You are also broad-minded and a progressive thinker with a predisposition to helping other knowledge-seekers. You would excel in the teaching profession. If you are to avoid nervous exhaustion, you must learn to pace yourself.

Inharmonious aspects

Persistence is often lacking here and you may give up too easily, forever looking for something new and different to investigate. Your challenge is to be less abrupt and tactless when dealing with those less gifted than you are.

Mercury to Neptune

Harmonious aspects

There is an indication here of some psychic abilities that you will want to explore. Allied to this are your highly developed intuition and the fantastic imagination that seem to pervade your everyday life. These skills need to be channeled, and some form of further education will show you the way.

Inharmonious aspects

Although you are extremely perceptive, you can also be naïve. Emotionally, too, you are ultra-sensitive. This can lead to self-deception, and you may not be above deceiving others. Your challenge is to stop worrying about your natural sensitivity and learn to control it.

Mercury to Pluto

Harmonious aspects

You are the flag bearer for honesty and fairness, being unable to tolerate any injustice in the world. However, you are also practical and down to earth. You are highly intuitive and you are well aware of this. Use your abilities to provide yourself with the answers to your own everyday problems as well as the problems of others.

Inharmonious aspects

You tend to be too intense, prone to jumping to conclusions without sufficient thought beforehand. Your challenge in life is to learn self-discipline, especially in your dealings with others.

Mercury to Ascendant

Harmonious aspects

You take pleasure in learning for its own sake, and enjoy discussion and debate. One reason for this is that you have the ability to express yourself easily and clearly. You have great creative potential, particularly in practical matters, and are never short of ideas for what to make next. Be aware that your ideas are so good that others may try to steal them.

Inharmonious aspects

For some reason, other people find it difficult to understand you. As a result, they tend to disregard what you say. Your challenge is to develop your own creative potential regardless of discouragement and criticism.

ASPECTS OF VENUS

Venus rules affection, what one values in others, personal possessions, personal money, beauty, sex, the feminine factor, women, mirrors, luxury, and having a good time.

Venus to Mars

Harmonious aspects

Your strong sex appeal is linked to an equally strong sexual drive, and you hate to be frustrated. Without an intimate relationship, you will be miserable and difficult. When you do find the perfect partner, you will both enjoy a harmonious relationship and indulge yourselves with luxuries, even though you may not be able to afford them.

Inharmonious aspects

Here your sexual drive becomes obsessive to the extent that you become impossible to live with. Your challenge here is to learn that cooperation and consideration is necessary in all spheres of life.

Venus to Jupiter

Harmonious aspects

There's nothing you like better than to help others. Therefore, you may find full-time employment in some aspect of caring service. This affection for others also translates to any partnerships, personal or professional, that you form, for they will be long and successful. You will never be truly happy until you have a comfortable home and enjoyable surroundings with good friends and a loyal partner.

Inharmonious aspects

You are too easy-going, and love the good life to the detriment of everything else. Your challenge is to control your extravagance.

Venus to Saturn

Harmonious aspects

These aspects are beneficial for all types of businesses, including partnerships. You are completely loyal to your many friends, though you may have difficulty forming and maintaining a closer, personal relationship. This is something that seems to elude you and you find it most frustrating, as you are accustomed to getting what you want.

Inharmonious aspects

Your relationships may become so difficult that you end up being friendless and lonely. Your challenge here must be to allow the free and full flow of your emotions.

Venus to Uranus

Harmonious aspects

You have a sensitive nature and are attracted to the finer things in life such as painting, music, poetry, and the performing arts. You have a feeling for humanitarian projects. Others see you as straightforward, genuine, and completely trustworthy. Your gregarious nature brings you many close friends.

Inharmonious relationships

You have problems forming relationships, often choosing unsuitable partners and, as a result, being easily led astray. Your challenge is to try to reduce your obsession with personal freedom.

Venus to Neptune

Harmonious aspects

Your ultra-sensitive nature leads you to delight in mystical, arcane, and esoteric studies and you will tend to look to them for inspiration. This may result in a conviction that a highly spiritual life is the only path that will lead you to enlightenment.

Inharmonious aspects

You may be confused emotionally, and possibly fantasize about an ideal love. This can only lead to disappointment. Your challenge must be to recognize your own delusions and plant your feet more firmly on the ground.

Venus to Pluto

Harmonious aspects

You have a passion for life and all that it has to offer, but you also need a trustworthy partner on whom to lavish your affection. You are very much aware of those members of society who are underprivileged and you will campaign long and hard on their behalf.

Inharmonious aspects

A tempestuous love life could be indicated here and social problems may arise as the result of traumatic relationships. Your challenge is to channel your passions into more tranquil and creative outlets.

Venus to Ascendant

Harmonious aspects

A happy domestic life is indicated here, which could be linked with a career partner. Your warm and enthusiastic qualities bring you friends and make you very popular. You are naturally outgoing and you try to be friendly with everyone you meet, never being judgmental or unkind. You are the archetypal diplomat and you would do well in a diplomatic profession.

Inharmonious aspects

Your preoccupation with pleasure may have a detrimental effect on your love life. Your challenge here is to learn how to express your emotions and to demonstrate your affection more clearly.

ASPECTS OF MARS

Mars rules drive, action, fighting for a cause, fighting for any reason, the way one attacks a problem or goes about a job, and stick-to-itiveness.

Mars to Jupiter

Harmonious aspects

You have the dual benefit of a freedom-loving nature and the capacity to live life to the full. This makes you a high-spirited person who puts a great deal of energy into all that you do. As a result, you usually achieve your objectives in life, even though they may seem highly ambitious by the standards of others.

Inharmonious aspects

You allow your enthusiasm to carry you away and are far too rash when important decisions need to be made. Your challenge in life is to recognize your extremist tendencies and learn to temper them.

Mars to Saturn

Harmonious aspects

You like a challenge, the bigger and more physical the better. You also have great organizational abilities and a strong practical streak. You are not the sort of person to pass up any worthwhile opportunities that come your way. Outside your professional life, you may become a master of some practical craft, which will serve you well in later years.

Inharmonious aspects

Your initial enthusiasm for projects is apt to wane so that you drift aimlessly from one scheme to another, achieving nothing. Your challenge is to learn to finish what you start.

Mars to Uranus

Harmonious aspects

You are full of initiative and drive that is revealed in practical and creative ways. Physical skills come easily to you. You are adept at anything that requires the use of your hands, from auto mechanics to plumbing to playing the flute. However, your intellectual approach and wide-ranging interests may draw you to fields of research and development, where you would also feel at home and do well.

Inharmonious aspects

You tend to let your ideas run away with you, becoming eccentric and irritable. Your challenge is to release your tension and learn to relax through physical activity.

Mars to Neptune

Harmonious aspects

These aspects are very favorable, increasing both your personal magnetism and your executive ability. Your natural warmth is sometimes hidden behind an apparent shyness, although this is merely a mask used to hide your deep feelings. You see only the best in others. In your private life, you are happy to ignore any failings in your partner in return for a peaceful life.

Inharmonious aspects

Your self-confidence evaporates all too easily when you are faced with difficulties. This, taken to extremes, can lead to health problems. Your challenge is to be aware of your true emotions and rely on them for strength.

Mars to Pluto

Harmonious aspects

With your dynamic attitude to life, you are a formidable opponent, being full of energy and emotion and well able to sell yourself and your ideas to others. You have the added advantage that you are always confident that you will succeed, and as a result, you usually do. You seek a partner who shares your high ideals and regard any physical attraction as being of lesser importance.

Inharmonious aspects

Your need for power may make you ruthless, unable to endure opposition. Your challenge in life is to learn how to establish harmonious relationships with other people.

Mars to Ascendant

Harmonious aspects

You have strong passions and emotions, which you demonstrate in an assertive and positive way. You are self-motivated and tend to act quite independently, ignoring even the best of well-intentioned advice. Nervous energy drives you on. Try to remember that self-discipline can mean restraining yourself rather than keeping your nose to the grindstone.

Inharmonious aspects

Your assertive nature can lead to aggression and you resent any interference, seeing slights—real or imaginary—as personal insults. Your challenge here is to learn to be less defensive and channel your energies creatively.

ASPECTS OF JUPITER

Jupiter rules higher education, belief systems, philosophy, religion, travel, foreigners, foreign places, and the law. Jupiter looks for barriers, and then transcends them.

Jupiter to Saturn

Harmonious aspects

You may think that you've become unglued occasionally, but you'll be extremely fortunate and land back on your feet before any damage is done. You lead a charmed life. To others you are a wealth of information.

Inharmonious aspects

You can't make up your mind whether to be ambitious or lazy. Unfortunately, your lack of enthusiasm often wins. Your challenge is to lower your sights a little and recognize that not everyone can reach the top.

Jupiter to Uranus

Harmonious aspects

You are an original thinker who is optimistic about the future, both on a personal level and for humankind. You are constantly planning new projects, but you are impatient to bring them about, quickly rejecting other people who are unwilling to accept your principles.

Inharmonious aspects

Tactlessness and a lack of self-confidence can lead you into many mistakes. Diplomacy is not your strong point. Your challenge is to hold your impulsive nature in check.

Jupiter to Neptune

Harmonious aspects

You are intensely philanthropic, but you have difficulty with the practicalities. Fortunately, your enthusiasm attracts the help of others to accomplish your charitable aims. You are particularly vulnerable to deception in your public and your private life. Beware of people who seek to use you only for their own ends.

Inharmonious aspects

You're extremely imaginative and apt to be gullible. Others will spot your weakness and prey on you if you allow it. Your challenge is to look before you leap in all areas of life.

Jupiter to Pluto

Harmonious aspects

Your deep moral and ethical convictions may lead you to seek seclusion. Your work for social reform and for less fortunate people makes you particularly suited to protect those who are not capable of defending themselves.

Inharmonious aspects

Any power you seek is intended solely for your own benefit. To this end, you are not above exploiting others or showing a complete lack of respect. Your challenge in life must be to recognize past failings and to reform.

Jupiter to Ascendant

Harmonious aspects

You are naturally philanthropic and generous, both with advice and with practical assistance. You find it almost impossible to refuse to help when it is asked of you, and this can be taken to extremes.

Inharmonious aspects

Over-indulgence is your main weakness. Your challenge is to modify your desires so that you fit into the society that you wish to embrace.

ASPECTS OF SATURN

Saturn rules old age, limitations, chronic sickness, and tribulations. However, it also represents roots, building blocks, structure, working with details and getting things right, respect, authority, and competence.

Saturn aspects are relevant to a group of people who were born during the same year. This is due to the length of time that it takes Saturn to obit the Sun and therefore, to traverse all twelve signs.

Saturn to Uranus

Harmonious aspects

You are a disciplined and patient person who has innovative ideas. You also have the capability to understand complex theories and then to communicate them to others so that they are clearly understood. You will do well in any field of learning, but especially in higher education where your skills will be most appreciated.

Inharmonious aspects

Your greatest difficulty is in making decisions, as you are completely conservative and hate diversification of any kind. Your challenge is to break with your old attachments and look forward, optimistically and positively, to the new.

Saturn to Neptune

Harmonious aspects

Your abilities seem limitless and you can achieve your high ideals. You have no difficulty in persuading others to give you assistance. You will be quite willing to put your love life on hold until later in life.

Inharmonious aspects

However hard you try, you are frustrated in your attempts to fulfill your dreams and tend to live a fantasy life. Your challenge in life is to keep your feet firmly on the ground.

Saturn to Pluto

Harmonious aspects

You are willing to try anything without fearing failure and you learn from mistakes that you make along the way. You are aware of the need for changes in society and see it as your duty to bring about such change.

Inharmonious aspects

You are a poor loser and are intimidated by anyone in a more powerful position than you. Your challenge is to be cautious in your dealings with others.

Saturn to Ascendant

Harmonious aspects

You tend to be a loner, only forming close relationships later in life. Your partners may be older than you are, as you have always had a great deal of respect for your seniors. You will take great care to avoid choosing the wrong partner, but you are happy to be independent, so you may well be content to go through life unattached.

Inharmonious aspects

You lack drive because you lack confidence, and you underestimate your own abilities. Your challenge is to be less of a perfectionist and more of a realist.

ASPECTS OF URANUS

Uranus is the breakout planet that rules change, revolution, originality, invention, and eccentricity. It also rules sudden and unexpected events. This outer planet takes many years to orbit the Sun, so it stays in each sign for several years. This means that Uranus's influence is a generational one that affects many people.

Uranus to Neptune

Harmonious aspects

You are broad-minded, understanding, and you see it as your duty in life to help others less gifted than yourself. Your attitude to religion or spiritual matters is ambivalent and you resist efforts to rule your thinking. You like to make up your own mind but do this only when you are sure that you have all the facts.

Inharmonious aspects

Your challenge in life is to find a positive outlet for your rebelliousness and avoid joining any organizations that have questionable motives.

Uranus to Pluto

Harmonious aspects

You bubble over with original ideas about the reformation of society, but your ideas change as you get older. You demand greater meaning in your life. The spirit world offers you a new dimension that you might decide to explore.

Inharmonious aspects

Hardships that come one after another seem to dog your life. Most will be outside your control, but your challenge is to make the best of things and to be careful not to allow others to hurt you.

Uranus to Ascendant

Harmonious aspects

Your enthusiasm and charismatic personality mean that you have many friends who willingly follow your intuitive leadership. The ace up our sleeve is your seemingly endless originality. Any disappointments you may have are liable to come from being let down by those you thought you could trust, especially in a personal relationship.

Inharmonious aspects

Your unpredictability makes you your own worst enemy. You are so keen on your own freedom and diversity that you never settle down to anything. Your challenge in life is to find a career in which you can exercise your freedom creatively.

ASPECTS OF NEPTUNE

Neptune rules dreams, vague desires, mysticism, glass (you can see through it as though it isn't there), the sea, water, anglers, film and film stars, fantasy, spiritual work, artistry and artistic work, music to some extent, and beauty. Oddly enough, Neptune can conceal but it can also reveal. This distant planet spends several years in each sign, so its influence is generational rather than personal.

Neptune to Pluto

All aspects

Neptune dissolves and Pluto transforms, so society is bound to change and be challenged when these two planets are in any kind of aspect.

Neptune to Ascendant

All aspects

On a personal level, easy aspects make it easy for you to express your kindness and your creativity. Challenging aspects make it hard for others to understand you. On a generational level, this brings changes in belief systems and sometimes a kind of collective madness.

ASPECTS OF PLUTO

Pluto rules hidden things, such as buried resentment, buried treasure, and mining. It also rules joining and parting, thus marriage, divorce, and the sharing or division of funds that come with these changes. It also rules sex, sexual magnetism, birth, and death—in short, all the big events that bring transformation. Pluto is a distant planet with a long orbit, so it affects a whole generation.

Pluto to Ascendant

Harmonious aspects

There is a powerful desire to transform society or to change the behavior of others—perhaps even whole countries or their religions and beliefs. Whether your generation pulls this off or not is a moot point.

Inharmonious aspects

You have great ideas, but go about implementing them in an unfortunate way. Others see you as being dictatorial and forever trying to dominate them. Your challenge is to direct your aggression toward outlets where competition is welcomed.

PISCES
ARIES
TAURUS
GEMINI
CANCER
LEO
VIRGO
LIBRA
SCORPIO
SAGITTARIUS
CAPRICORN
AQUARIUS

Chart Interpretation

9

It is quite difficult and time-consuming to construct your own chart. Whole books are written on this topic alone. Chart construction involves many complex calculations, including the use of logarithms, and any one mistake, easily made and not easily spotted, will result in a flawed chart. Calculating your own chart by hand can be complicated, and we consider it outside the scope of the "plain and simple" approach of this book

Nowadays the ordeal of do-it-yourself has been removed with the advent of computers and astrological software that will calculate your chart in a flash. Go online, look for astrology software firms, and peruse their products' features to see what they have to offer. Some software is only suitable for professional or research astrologers and it is much too complex and expensive for a beginner. You need only reasonably priced program for most basic requirements.

Several websites exist that will provide you with a chart free of charge. One is called Astrodienst (*www.astro.com*). You have only to key in your birth details—date, place, and exact time—and your chart will be calculated for you. You can download charts and even obtain a good character reading from this service; several options are free of charge.

If you don't have a computer, you can go to your local library or a computer café, or ask a friend who can access the Internet, or pay a visit to your neighborhood astrologer.

Making a Start on Interpretation

One you have a chart prepared, there are several steps to take to interpret it. The steps involved are

1. Check the ascendant (see page 69)
2. Check the Sun sign (see page 3)
3. Check the Moon sign (see page 81)
4. Check out each planet by sign (see page 45)
5. Check out each planet by house (see page 95)
6. Check the genders (see page 37)
7. Check the elements (see page 37)
8. Check the qualities (see page 37)
9. Check the aspects, one by one (see page 107)

Let's look at our sample chart, which is for Hollywood superstar, Denzel Washington. Denzel was born on December 28, 1954, at Mount Vernon, New York, at 9 minutes after midnight (00:09) Eastern Standard Time.

Here is Denzel Washington's birth chart.

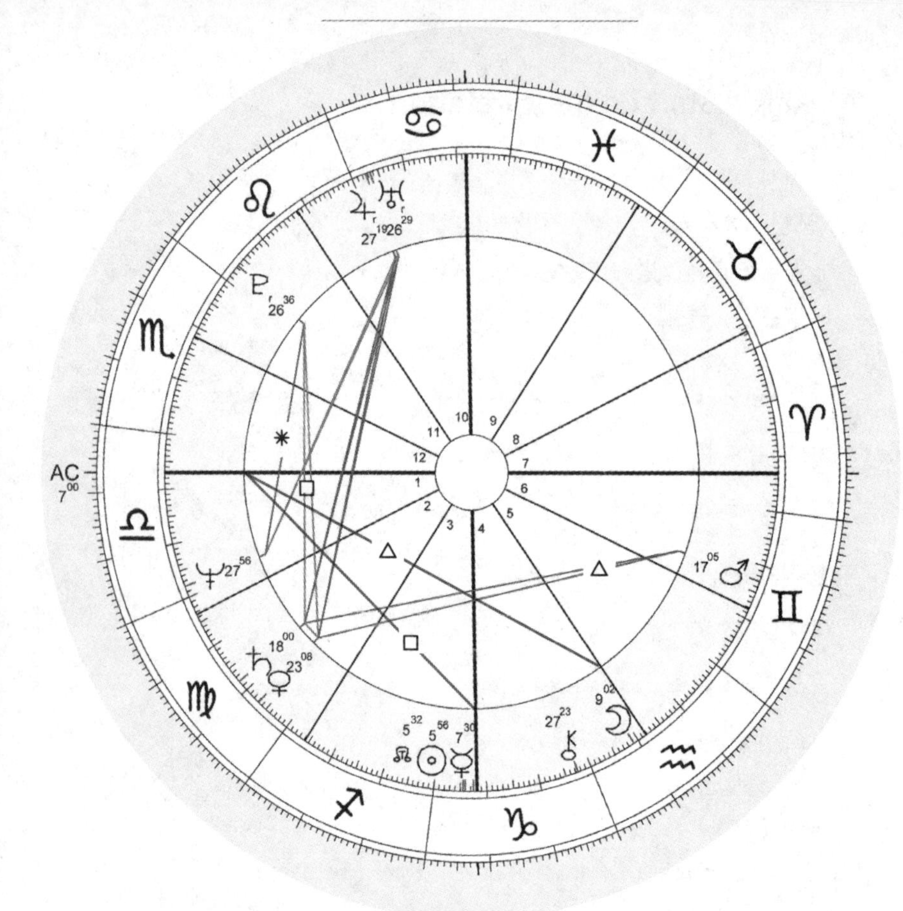

Planet	Sign it occupies	House it occupies
Sun ☉	Capricorn ♑	3
Moon ☽	Aquarius ♒	5
Mercury ☿	Capricorn ♑	3
Venus ♀	Scorpio ♏	2
Mars ♂	Pisces ♓	6
Jupiter ♃	Cancer ♋	10
Saturn ♄	Scorpio ♏	2
Uranus ♅	Cancer ♋	10
Neptune ♆	Libra ♎	1
Pluto ♇	Leo ♌	11

The first thing to look for in a chart is the rising sign (ascendant), always on the left-hand side. Looking at Denzel's chart, we see that the AC glyph (symbol) on the outer ring is in the sign of Libra. This shows that Denzel has 7 degrees and 34 minutes of Libra as his exact ascendant. For our purposes, it is enough to say that Denzel's ascendant is 7 degrees of Libra.

Next, look for the Sun, which you will see at the bottom of the chart at 5 degrees and 56 minutes of Capricorn. As there are only 59 minutes in a degree, you could say that Denzel's Sun is 6 degrees Capricorn. The spokes of the inner circle delineate the houses, and counting from the ascendant in a counter-clockwise direction, you'll see that the Sun is in the third house.

Next, look to see where the planets are placed. You'll find all the planets listed as glyphs in Denzel's chart, but we've saved you the eyestrain of interpreting them by listing them here for you beneath the chart.

In the very center circle of this chart, you will notice a bunch of straight lines traversing from one house to another. In the middle of these lines are little symbols: these symbols indicate the aspects. Depending on the angle of these lines, aspects can be easy or hard, beneficial, harmonious, or difficult. Aspects represent where problems, challenges, and opportunities lie. You can use the descriptions in chapter 8 to interpret Denzel's aspects.

Now that you have all the nuts-and-bolts planets and placement laid out, it's good to get the overall picture by assessing the gender, elements, and the qualities in Denzel's chart.

The listing that follows shows you the situation for all the planets and the ascendant.

Genders

Masculine	Feminine
3	7

Elements

Fire	Earth	Air	Water
1	2	2	5

Qualities

Cardinal	Fixed	Mutable
5	4	1

Denzel Washington has lovely Libra rising. This gives him his charm and good looks. On its own, Libra rising is a nice facet, but the addition of Venus in Scorpio and even, perhaps, Saturn in Scorpio makes him downright charismatic and sexy!

Denzel has more feminine planets than masculine ones. This speaks to the fact that he is an actor rather than a fighter or a business tycoon.

Denzel has three planets each in intellectual air and emotional water signs, so he can emote powerfully on the silver screen, and he uses his brains while doing so. Two planets in earth signs help to make him practical, so he may be a good person to call when you need a shelf put up! Having only one planet in fire slows Denzel down and perhaps adds to his laid-back attitude rather than the kind of hyperactive attitude that a more fiery personality would display. Pluto is his only planet in a fire sign. Pluto with its long orbit is a planet of slow transformation, so this placement shows that his enthusiasms (fire) don't come and go willy-nilly. Denzel finds what he wants to achieve, and only makes changes toward that goal slowly and deliberately.

With five planets in cardinal signs, Denzel is more than capable of getting his own way. This is a very forceful personality wrapped up in a charming package. The four planets in fixed signs make Denzel dig in once he has his mind made up. The only flexibility that he displays comes from his one mutable planet, but that is Mars in Pisces. He can take two different approaches to a role or to any artistic endeavor, but once he has decided which one is right for him, he will not be persuaded to change his mind. In short, he's a tough cookie in a lovely package.

Now look at his placements of Sun in Capricorn, Moon in Scorpio, and Libra rising. Going back to chapter 2 and chapter 4 in this book, read the descriptions of these signs, and the descriptions of these planets. Think about how the energies of each planet blends with the sign of the zodiac where it is positioned. Then look at the houses that these planets occupy, and see how the energies of each house would affect the energy of the planet, and the energy of the sign (see the table on page 105 for a quick guide to key-words for each house).

The trick with chart interpretation is to combine the energy of the planet with the nature of the sign and then with the area of life that the house deals with.

Looking at Denzel's chart, here is an example of how to interpret one of his placements by planet, sign, and house:

Saturn (work, responsibility) in Scorpio (intuitive, secretive) in the second house (home, security): The fact that Saturn is in the second house shows that it took time for Denzel to find the right image for his work and for himself as a person. It will have taken him time to accumulate the wealth that he enjoys but once he has done so, he will do his best to hang on to it (Scorpio). The second house is about values, and with Saturn there, Denzel values putting in an effort, attending to details, and doing his duty. He also values other people who take the same attitude. He is likely to spend a fair bit of his wealth on his parents (Saturn can represent either parent according to different astrology systems). This placement suggests that Denzel's parents were a considerable support to him and one parent or even grandparent was a powerful role model who Denzel looked admired.

Saturn is conjunct Venus (see chapter 8, The Aspects). Some people are very lucky in their marriages, partnerships, and other relationship with this placement, but others find it a dampener on love. Denzel seems to have a good family life, though. Saturn is also trine Mars and in a wide trine to Uranus. This means that he can use his drive (Mars) and uniqueness (Uranus) to obtain the status, respect and wealth (Saturn) that he wants.

Denzel's complete list of aspects is as follows:

Sun conjunct ☌ Mercury
Sun square □ ascendant
Moon trine △ ascendant
Venus trine △ Mars
Venus trine △ Jupiter
Venus conjunct ☌ Saturn
Venus trine △ Uranus
Venus square □ Pluto
Mars trine △ Saturn
Jupiter trine △ Uranus
Jupiter square □ Neptune
Uranus square □ Neptune
Neptune square □ Pluto

As you did with the planets and signs, go into the chapter on aspects and look up these characteristics one by one. For example, Denzel has Sun conjunct Mercury. This indicates he will almost certainly be strong-willed, with a high intellect.

Deciphering a birth chart can take some time since it involves a blending of information. Now that we know Denzel has Sun conjunct Mercury, let's see what else we can discover about this aspect.

Looking at his chart and his list of planets, signs, and houses, we see that the Sun is conjunct Mercury in the third house, in the sign of Capricorn.

Going back to page 51 in this book, we find that Mercury is the planet connected with communication of all kinds, with your friends and siblings, and with the way that your mind works.

Going back to page 29 in this book, we find that Capricorn is sure-footed, and cerebral. There's nothing indecisive about Capricorn—this is a very self-disciplined individual, able to plan and achieve long-term goals—the possibility of failure simply does not exist for Denzel.

Finally, going to page 100 in this book, we find that the third house is associated with our immediate environment and the way we communicate within it. The third house is concerned with day-to-day contacts—for Denzel, most likely this will show how well he relates to his co-stars.

Blending these elements together—sign, planet, house, aspect—gives us the fullest picture possible of Denzel.

When you begin your journey into chart interpretation, start with your own chart. You know yourself better than anyone, and as you blend together the interpretations for sign, planet, house, and aspect, only you will be able to know if it "rings true."

Predictive Techniques: Interpreting the Transit Chart

Professional astrologers can choose from a number of techniques for predicting the future, but this book is called *Astrology Plain and Simple*, so let's keep things simple and use a technique that every astrologer knows: a technique is called *transits*.

This is taking things a bit farther than most beginning astrology books do, but transits are not that difficult to do, and most people love to make predictions. Have you ever picked up your local paper (or even your phone app!) to check your horoscope for the day? That information is based on transits.

The word "horoscope" means "map of the hour." The birth chart represents a sky map for the time of birth, but the stars are always moving—they are in *transit*. So if you want to see what's coming your way in the near future, you have to take a few extra steps. Let's say you're getting married on June 20 of a particular year. In such a case, you want to look at a specific time and a specific place. The easiest thing to do is to just have a new chart calculated with the "birth time" of your wedding. However, most astrologers use predictive techniques to look at trends that are occurring over a few weeks or months because it takes the planets varying amounts of time to travel through—or "transit"—each sign. In this case, you would draw those new planetary placements outside the ring of the original birth chart. Once that is done, you can compare the new transiting planets against the original birth planets, making note of the aspects they are making.

Let us return to Denzel Washington for the moment. As an example, back in 2005 when we were studying Denzel's chart, we decided that we wanted to see what would happen to Denzel in the early part of 2007, so we calculated a new chart for March 1, 2007, which we show you on page 158.

Once we had drawn up the new chart, we took the planets from that and put them *outside the original birth chart*. Now I can use all the knowledge I have learned from this book about the nature of planets, signs, houses, and aspects to see what is going on in Denzel's 2007 life.

This section will give you an idea of the information that can be gleaned once you learn to interpret transits. We'll take each feature one by one, just as we did when looking at the birth chart.

The Transiting Ascendant

The new ascendant moves very quickly and it will move right around the chart within the space of 24 hours. Unless Denzel had an important meeting, interview, or date on a particular day that was set for a particular time, we wouldn't bother to examine the transiting ascendant at all. As it happens, in this example you will see transiting ascendant was at 9 degrees of Leo and in the eleventh house.

The Transiting Sun

The transiting Sun is at 10 degrees of Pisces. Denzel's natal Mars is at 17 degrees of Pisces. The Sun moves quickly (a touch under a degree per day) so it is clear that in about a week's time, Denzel will have a Sun/Mars transit. This could set him off in flurry of activity, or he may lose his temper at that time. He should take

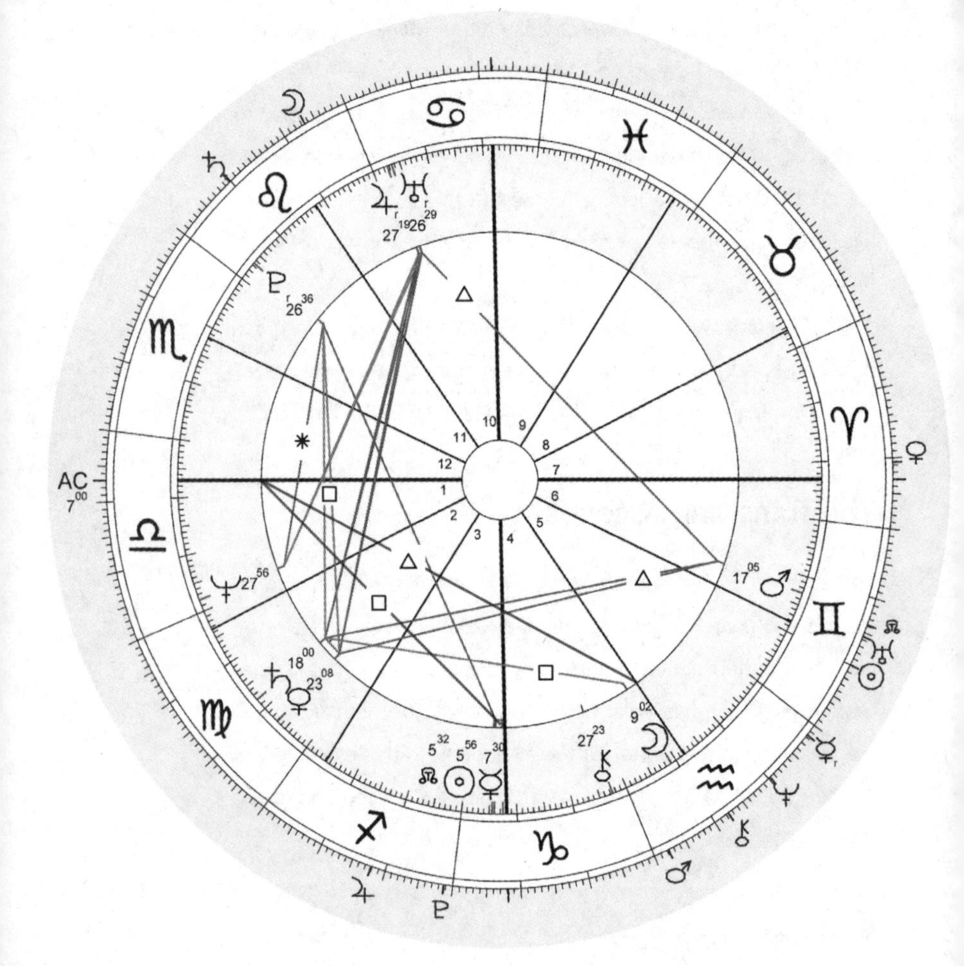

AC
7 00
10
9
11
8
12
7
1
6
2
5
3
4
26 36
27 19 26 29
27 56
17 05
18 00
23 08
5 32
5 56
7 30
27 23
9 02

care when driving or operating machinery. The fact that all this is happening in Pisces makes it less fearsome, since Pisces is a gentle water sign. The events will take place in the sixth house, so Denzel will be very active (and maybe angry) at work. As this house relates to health and to the head, he may have a headache or eyestrain on that day.

The Transiting Moon

Like the transiting ascendant, the Moon moves so quickly that it is only worth looking at this for an event at a specific time. In this example, the transiting Moon was at 16 degrees of Leo.

Transiting Mercury

This is at 27 degrees of Aquarius in Denzel's fifth house. Mercury also moves very quickly, at a little more than a degree per day, so it will be out of Aquarius within a couple of days. Meanwhile, this will bring a few original ideas to Denzel, and he will apply these to his leisure activities, his creativity, his children, and family, to gambling, making vacation plans, playing sport, or to lovemaking (all fifth house activities). Meanwhile, note that transiting Mercury is separating from an opposition to Pluto. This could represent a power struggle of some kind relating to creative work. Denzel might have been up against a tax deadline, a corporation, or even his wife regarding his ideas (Mercury rules the mentality) or those of others. He might be arguing with one of his children (fifth house) even yelling at them to turn the music (fifth house) down, and to stop spending money (Pluto) on their friends (eleventh house). Lots of options there, no? However, Mercury moves so quickly that its effects are unlikely to be long-lasting.

Transiting Venus

Venus is also fast-moving, but for the moment, it is at 10 degrees of Aries and in the seventh house, so Denzel is taking an active role in partnerships, love, and marriage, or joint ventures of some kind. That would fit Venus transiting active, fiery Aries in the seventh house.

Transiting Mars

Mars moves more slowly, taking about two years to move through the complete zodiac. For the moment, it is in Aquarius and because it is only 2 degrees right now, it will be in that sign for a couple of months yet. Now, Mars is transiting the fourth house, suggesting that Denzel is putting his energies into his home and family situation. It will soon move to the fifth house of creativity, so no doubt he will soon be back at work, putting his energies into making something of his next project. In a week or so, Mars will conjunct the Moon. This could send Washington household into a flurry of family activity, bringing fun and good company to the house.

Transiting Jupiter

For this year (2007), Jupiter is in Sagittarius and in Denzel's third house. This could take him on quite a voyage of mental exploration. If he works on a film, the action might take place in some far-off location and Denzel will learn much about some foreign place. [Editor's note: During this time, Denzel was wrapping up *American Gangster*, filmed in the United States and Thailand; a film which won numerous accolades and awards.] Everything relating to Jupiter will be emphasized by its presence in its own sign of Sagittarius and in a house that has a similarly explorative energy. He could become involved with contracts and other legal matters and he may find a new philosophy during this period.

Transiting Saturn

This is a little worrying as Saturn is a slow-moving planet and it is already beginning to come into a conjunction with Pluto. By the time this is over, which could take several months, Saturn and Pluto will have brought some serious pain Denzel's way. This is all happening in Leo and in the eleventh house, so it could relate to sad news about his or some other relatives' children (Leo) or friends (eleventh house). A hoped for project (eleventh house) could be too grandiose (Leo) to make it to fruition.

Transiting Saturn is also about to square natal Venus, and to reinforce the natal square between Venus and Pluto. This will put some real strain on Denzel's relationships and it could lead to some real misunderstandings.

Transiting Neptune

Neptune really does take its time, so its effects last for a year or two in some cases. It is coming into an opposition with Pluto and a square to Venus. This will represent a real muddle. If Denzel is doing anything he shouldn't, it will come out into the open now! Neptune has spent several years in Aquarius and it has a few more to go yet, so its effects on Denzel's friendships (Aquarius) and his creativity and leisure (fifth house) are quite strange. He could have some kind of psychic revelation or turn to a different way of looking at life, and bring that into his work. Neptune rules film, and the fifth house rules entertainment, so we definitely have not seen the last of this charismatic actor.

Transiting Pluto

This is at 28 degrees of Sagittarius and it is making a trine to Denzel's natal Pluto and a sextile to natal Neptune. Pluto only moves a degree or two in a year, so these aspects are likely to affect Denzel over a long period, so it is just as well that they are harmonious aspects.

Pluto in the third house in Sagittarius leads Denzel into more marketing of his skills than ever, and possibly also into writing (the third house concerns writing, while Sagittarius relates to publishing). His wealth will increase, and apart from one or two minor setbacks, he seems set for many good years to come!

ABOUT THE AUTHORS

Cass Jackson was head of a large grammar school when he started to write. As a part-time freelance writer, he produced short stories for magazines and for boys' comics. At the same time, he was developing his interest in complementary therapies and New Age subjects, eventually qualifying as a Reiki master, herbalist, and astrologer. (He's also a registered goldsmith and silversmith!) He quit teaching and became editor of a small motoring magazine. Cass also became director of studies for an international correspondence course on writing for children, and he produced several books on various aspects of writing. This led to several writing jobs, the launch of Cass and Janie's own magazine, and the establishment of residential courses.

Janie Jackson has worked in some form of writing and publishing all her life. She has worked on magazines and newspapers, as staff, in public relations, or as a features writer. She has taught writing in adult education colleges, and along with Cass, has run various courses for writers.

Cass and Janie have written seven books on various mind, body, and spirit subjects and have edited several more for various publishers. Both are astrologers and both are interested in healing, complementary health, and psychology.

Hampton Roads Publishing Company

...for the evolving human spirit